# Real
# Merthyr

# Real
# Merthyr

## Mario Basini

seren

Seren is the book imprint of
Poetry Wales Press Ltd
Nolton Street, Bridgend, Wales
**www.seren-books.com**

© Mario Basini, 2008

The right of Mario Basini to be identified
as the Author of this Work
has been asserted in accordance with the
Copyright, Designs and Patents Act, 1988.

ISBN 978-1-85411-482-2

A CIP record for this title is available from
the British Library

The publisher works with the financial assistance
of the Welsh Books Council

Printed by Bell & Bain, Glasgow

# CONTENTS

## WEST

## SOUTH

## CENTRAL 2

# INTRODUCTION

This isn't one of those simple places. No quiet origins as a fishing village: too far from the coast; or a market town: for whom? Not built on a hill fort. Not the site of a great battle or a commanding castle at the confluence of rivers. Not built where the weather was kind and the sun always shone and the vines grew in profusion. No town full of glovemakers, or tailors, or armourers, or mystics, or sailors. Instead named twice. Martyr Tudfyl. Site of the slaying of the daughter of the Prince of Brycheiniog, in times when the sky was dark and nothing was written down. Merthyr Tudfyl. Merthyr and Tydfil. The town still retains those two separate words. Never simplified like Barry, Bangor, Bala or Brynna. Never compressed, Germanically, like Caerdydd, Caernarfon, Aberystwyth, Aberbargoed, Abertyleri and Pontlottyn. Merthyr Tydfil. Distinct and twofold like Milford Haven and Builth Wells. In Wales there are not many of those.

Merthyr, town of iron. Full of myths. You can list these. Largest concentration of poets anywhere in Wales. Shortest people in Western Europe. Highest incidence of heart disease. More rainfall than anywhere south of Pen y Fan. Entirely socialist. Always republican. Vibrant. Never used as a setting for *Torchwood*. No millionaires. Fewest remaining ancient buildings. Those who work here don't live here. Best curry anywhere in the cymric diaspora. Original site for the new Welsh Assembly, the revitalised Arts Council and the high-tech South Wales Police Headquarters. Didn't get any of those. Once twinned with Clichy-la-Garenne, north Paris. Not any more.

Factory outlets at Dowlais. Asda on the hill. The rising green of the Beacons to the north. The coalfield and its scars and twisted valleys running away south.

Famous for Johnny Owen, Howard Winstone and Eddie Thomas, fighters. Laura Ashley, flowers. Philip Madoc, thespian. Joseph Parry, composer of 'Myfanwy'. Bill Roberts who built the first dalek. Larry Love, singer for the Alabama 3 whose voice we've all heard accompanying Tony Soprano as he used to drive each week along the turnpike at Jersey. Leslie Norris was born here. There's a memorial plaque at the library. Jack Jones made the town world-known in his fiction. Not a bad total for a municipality of only 55,000. The late historian Gwyn Alf Williams explained the town's place as epicentre of industrial Britain and the true focus of socialist working man for the whole wide world. I was once taken on a guided tour with Gwyn around the town centre. Took an eternity. Everyone we passed, he knew, and they all stopped to chat.

Among the writers, Glyn Jones was an early champion. Born at 16 Clare Street, went to Cyfarthfa School. A school in a castle. Merthyr's pretty unique in having that. The late Charles Jones stopped people in the streets to sell them his hand-made books of poetry. Mike Jenkins, still very much alive, encapsulates the unique local voice in his stories and vernacular verse. Harri Webb, Meic Stephens and Peter Gruffydd lived here, at the long demolished Garth Newydd. Lady Charlotte Guest made the *Mabinogion* accessible with her English translation, created at Dowlais House, gone now. Des Barry was born here as his rip-roaring novel, *A Bloody Good Friday*, shows. Rachel Trezise came chasing the local heavy metal bands. Raging lead guitar and cans of ale. Lots. Is there a decent bookshop here? A valley's Waterstones or Borders? Nope.

The Romans built a fort at Penydarren, side of their road north, to guard against the roaring Welsh. You can find it today under the football ground. The Normans arrived and built a castle at Morlais to subdue the natives. Same story all over South Wales. But the big change came five-hundred years later when industrial Britain turned to iron and steam. Merthyr's big story stems almost entirely from that. Largest industrial conurbation in the western world, four iron works, smoke and slag and fire enough to make capitalist master-thieves of the owners and their supporters and all the men who lived in the big houses and whose hands never touched dirt. But enough distress and poverty to wear out a people. And what a people. They came from Wales, the north, the west, from Ireland, from the west of England, from Italy, from Germany, and from further afield in their droves. Merthyr became a crucible of change, a tiger of gold and dirt, a place of great fire, coal and wealth on the edge of an empty Welsh world.

Most of that's gone now. All of that's gone. The works closed, the railways ripped, the canal filled in. All that remains is the track up from Merthyr Vale. Commuters use the line to reach Merthyr town, those who work here. Youth take it back down to the party-lands and vertical drinkeries of the Cardiff south. You can track the town's history, pick up pieces of it in the street. I've had that done for me. Been shown where China was, where the works stood, where the canal went and the rail reached, where the coal came from, where the triangle was before demolition, and the Lamb, all that. You can track it but not see it. Today it's memory only. History wiped.

At the unveiling of a plaque to the memory of the great Merthyr author Leslie Norris at the library we get speeches. Meic Stephens from the Rhys Davies Trust, Cary Archard reading Leslie's fluid poetry, and the Mayor telling us how Merthyr is proud. The small crowd of onlookers applaud. On the walk back to the Mayor's parlour (first floor of the almost brutalist Council Offices, back of Castle Street) the Mayor points out sites of interest – memorials, locations of resurrections, the place where pubs once stood. Touchable history may be gone but its traces remain near the surface. In the parlour, with its wide sun-filled windows, we get tea and Merthyr biscuits. Look back out towards the bus station at all the smokeless silence. In 1831 the Merthyr Rising took place here. The red flag flew. Dic Penderyn wounded a soldier, so it was said, and was hanged for doing so. Another martyr was made and no one has ever forgotten. Merthyr is not like other places.

In the Dental Hospital waiting for treatment I read through the manuscript you now hold as a published book. What you reading, asked the nurse. I thought I recognised the accent, how could I not. You from Merthyr? I am. There's a coincidence. This is *Real Merthyr*, a great book about the town by Mario Basini. An Italian! What's an Italian doing writing about Merthyr? Doing it well, I told her. Born in the town. As were more of his countrymen than you'd imagine. Knows the place backwards. *Real Merthyr* by Mario Basini, journalist, author. A new way of looking at one of the world's most historically vibrant places. You'll enjoy it when it comes out. You will.

Mario Basini's *Real Merthyr* is the latest in the series of Seren's *Real* books. It's written to the same formula created by the highly successful *Real Cardiff*. History, topography, reminiscence, psycho-geography. Another way of looking at things. A real way.

Peter Finch
May 2008

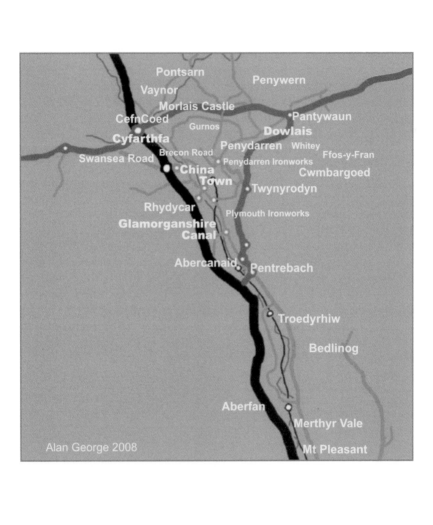

# NORTH

## DOWLAIS TOP

Below me as I stand in the car park of a superstore this bright, cold February afternoon, the traffic flows ceaselessly through the cancer of round-abouts that sweeps the Heads of the Valleys Road past the northern tip of Merthyr. Each year the tarmac eats further into the bleak beauty of the blaenau, the high moorland from which half a dozen rivers, among them the Taff, the Ebbw and the Rhondda, spring to score out their narrow valleys. Each year the flow of vehicles thickens to fill the new space available to it.

The cars and thundering trucks speed east to Abergavenny and the English Midlands, south to Cardiff, west to Neath, Swansea and rural Wales. Only an odd bus or a taxi turns into the narrow mouth of Dowlais, scorned and neglected like a mistress whose sagging beauty now repels her former lovers. What was a crowded, vital town of 18,000 people, Merthyr's twin, is shrunk to a village a third of that size. It bears the desultory air of a community by-passed by history. The quiet of terraced streets bathed in a wintry sun is punctuated by a languid bark from a row of breeding kennels. Youths spread hay in a field for their horses. Woodsmoke from a garden fire scents the air. A man hoes his neat allotment purposefully, nostalgic for the work that once gave focus to his life. Dowlais, the proudest and most dynamic of the iron- and steel-making communities that made up Merthyr Tydfil, is returning, exhausted, to its pre-industrial innocence.

Two hundred years ago it was very different. Artists, journalists and aristocratic tourists flocked here to gawp at the wonder of the new industrial world, the sprawling ironworks that clamoured for miles along the valley floor. They came to see the pot-bellied furnaces spew out their streams of molten iron and turn the air into a fire which singed the hair off your skin. They came to gasp at the heart-stopping skills of the puddlers, their bare torsos liquid with sweat as they manipulated the white-hot metal with their long tongs as if it was a harmless twist of toffee.

They came to hear the pounding of engines and steam hammers, of baying horses and men bellowing commands or warnings. They came to taste the smoke, acrid as ammonia, that belched from chimneys into a mountain air once pristine with birdsong. They came to watch ragged lines of women and children, wrapped, Eskimo-like, in protective hats and gloves, toil in the brickworks or among a rats-tails' tangle of rails and trucks filled with jagged, razor-sharp chunks of iron ore, limestone and coal. Above all, they came to see the vision of hell conjured by the mountains of molten waste produced by a works about to become the biggest in the world. The incandescent slag tips and furnace mouths turned night into day, a mocking inversion of nature that filled the onlooker with wonder at man's audacity.

Some were tourists drawn by nothing more than a wish to see the sights. So in 1802 a coach containing British history's most notorious ménage-a-trois bumped and clattered along the track that is now the Heads of the Valleys Road. Inside were England's greatest military hero, the one-armed, one-eyed Nelson; his lover, the plump and blowsy Lady Emma Hamilton; and her comfortable Welsh cuckold, the ageing sybarite Sir William. They visited Dowlais's great rival, the Cyfarthfa Ironworks two miles down the valley. Cyfarthfa produced many of the canon in Nelson's navy, including those on his flagship, The *Victory*.

At Cyfarthfa, they were greeted by its fat, trigger-tempered owner, Richard Crawshay, a Yorkshireman who epitomised the energy, the arrogance and the indifference to human suffering of the early ironmasters. As Nelson and his entourage entered the works Crawshay, sensing his Welsh workers' lack of a proper respect, glared at them and bellowed, "Cheer, you buggers". They obeyed, fearful no doubt of his capricious power that in an instant could turf them out of work and into destitution.

Fifty years before, Merthyr had been at the heart of an unhurried but thriving rural community of hill farmers and cottage craftsmen specialising in weaving, stone-cutting, carpentry and clock-making. In 1723, the journalist, novelist, intrepid traveller and government spy, Daniel Defoe, had been so intimidated by the wild grandeur of an area "mountainous to an extremity …looking so full of horror that we thought to have given over our enterprise and left Wales out of our circuit." Even he was forced to admit that Merthyr occupied "a most agreeable vale opening to the south, with a pleasant river running through it called the Taafe."

The handful of men about to transform this idyll into the fire and brimstone forge of the industrial revolution arrived, rubbing hard to bring life back into their numb buttocks, after a backbreaking journey on horseback across a wild mountain track from Cardiff. They were English merchants, entrepreneurs, engineers and ironmakers from the west Midlands where the industry had already flamed into life. The Crawshays, the Guests, the Hills, the Homfrays were hard-drinking, hard-gambling hard-men, prepared to drive themselves to the limit of endurance in their hungry pursuit of wealth, and the men, women and children they employed beyond it.

They had been drawn to Merthyr because it possessed everything they needed for iron-making: an abundance of wood and coal to fire their furnaces, and iron ore and limestone to feed them. By the time of Nelson's visit they had established four great ironworks – at Pentrebach to the south of Merthyr, Cyfarthfa to the west, Penydarren to the north east and Dowlais, two miles north of that. Cyfarthfa and Dowlais would in turn become the biggest in the world. Each works bred its own community. Each community had its distinctive ethnic make-up and culture. Immigrants from the rest of Wales clustered in areas where their neighbours had settled. Penydarren became the home of a colony of Shropshire men, imported for their iron-making skills. When, under the pressures of expansion, they merged into one another along the valley floor, they kept their individuality and insularity. Growing up in Penydarren, two miles south of the centre of Dowlais, I could count on the fingers of one hand the number of times I visited the town which still boasted most of the 18,000 people which once crowded it. Even when I went to a school just within its southern border, Dowlais remained as remote to me as Timbuktu.

Within a century of the arrival of those first ironmasters, Merthyr and Dowlais had exploded into Wales's biggest town, together boasting 50,000 people. Some came from the English counties bordering South Wales: Herefordshire, Gloucestershire and Somerset. Most arrived from rural Wales: Carmarthenshire, Pembrokeshire,

Breconshire. They were driven by the poverty of life on the farm and by the promise of wages so good not even the threat of death or terrible injury in the furnaces, nor of the deadly diseases bred in insanitary streets, could deter them. From the first, industrial Merthyr attracted an exotic smattering of foreigners. In 1845, for example, the *Cardiff and Merthyr Guardian* noted the court case in which a man from Calcutta claimed he had been robbed of £2 by his girlfriend. Five years later, a black American labourer, Theodore Johnson, 23, was found guilty of robbing a man in one of the town's most notorious red light districts and transported "beyond the sea" for 10 years. At his request, half of the jury at Johnson's trial at the Glamorgan Assizes in Cardiff consisted of foreigners. It included "French, Genoese, Prussian, Hebrew, English and Welsh". Merthyr already boasted colonies of Irish labourers, English craftsmen and Russian and Polish street traders. Spanish ironworkers, Chinese laundrymen and Italian street entertainers and café owners would quickly follow.

## TWYN-Y-WAUN AND PANTYWAUN

The empty road ribbons towards hump-backed hills rising like dolphins to the horizon. Their slopes turn green and gold and violet as the light, filtered through scudding clouds, dances across them. A village at their feet bleaches in the sun. This bleak moorland on the roof of the valley to the east of Dowlais is deserted now, apart from the sheep and a few cows nuzzling the brown grass fruitlessly. But once it was a meeting place as important to the life of Merthyr as the Forum was for Rome. The reedy, ankle-breaking hummocks of Twyn-y-Waun hosted an annual fair that stretched back to medieval times. Men and their wives traded horses, bought cures off quacks, got drunk, bayed as bareknuckle mountain fighters pulped each other, fought and made love. Here, during the outbursts of violent protest that pockmarked Merthyr's early industrial history, mobs of workers gathered to hide from pursuing soldiers, to lick their wounds and to listen to their leaders, summoning their wills for the next battle.

This bare land was once the placenta that nourished the infant industrial Merthyr. It is studded with the spoil tips of old iron ore mines, coal pits and abandoned limestone quarries. Tramroads and railway lines networked the moors to feed the ironworks and their communities. Villages clustering against the howling winds, the driving rain and the blizzards, housed miners, colliers and quarry-men. Most have now disappeared, like Pantywaun, scooped up and dumped into history by the open-cast excavators. Built in the late eighteenth century by the Dowlais ironworks to house its workers, it was a modest collection of forty families, a railway halt, a couple of pubs, a chapel, a church and a mission hall. Close and self-reliant, its people spoke Welsh long after the language had been abandoned by Dowlais two miles away.

Pantywaun's cocoon of insularity exploded one winter's night in 1865 when a stranger staggered out of a snow storm and collapsed, half-dead, on the street. On his back he carried a heavy wooden cabinet which contained a mechanical barrel-organ. Beneath his coat huddled a bewildered, freezing monkey on whom his master lavished as much attention as he on did himself. The organ-grinder was carried to the nearest public house where he found a clean bed and a new life.

His name would be variously recorded by registrars and census takers in the ensuing years as Domic Beigaelio, Domic Seisseiglas, Dominick Bassiglio and Domic Basalgeao. An illiterate – he signed the birth certificate of his daughter Isabella with an "X" – he was in no position to correct them. But he was almost certainly called Domenico Bacigalupo, a surname as popular in his part of Italy as Williams or Jones in Wales. He had arrived in London five years earlier to make a living as an organ-grinder. Occasionally, driven out of the city by the number of entertainers crowding its streets, he would leave on a short tour to find new customers prepared to pay a

copper to hear his out-of-tune repertoire of songs, marches and operatic arias while his monkey, splendid in his scarlet uniform, collected the money in his hat, or clambered up the facades of houses to snatch coins from the hands of those watching at upstairs windows.

Young and vigorous with an aura of the exotic, Domenico proved irresistible to at least one local girl. Mary Jones was a desirable catch destined for someone much higher up the social ladder than an itinerant street musician. She belonged to a well-known family of chemists and herbalists based in nearby Aberdare. Her father, an entrepreneur who supplied iron ore to the Dowlais works, was understandably unhappy with the match. But his daughter's determination, bolstered perhaps by the fact she was already pregnant, forced his approval of their marriage. He found Domenico a job as a miner in a nearby Dowlais company colliery.

The couple moved to a little house in Coedcae Row at the top of Dowlais. It still stands, its entrance porch set back from the road as if it has been added as an afterthought. Domenico and Mary produced nine children, the eldest of whom, John Martin 'Basagelao', showed the entrepreneurial spirit he inherited from both his parents. He became a property developer, buying first the public house, The Tredegar Arms, which still stands just across the road from where his parents had lived.

Mary was a strong-minded woman determined to run their home the way she wanted. A devout Baptist, she did make some concessions to her husband's Roman Catholicism. She allowed him to go to mass in St Illtyd's, the first Catholic church in the Valleys which had opened in Dowlais twenty years earlier. She even provided a pony and trap so he could make the brief journey of a mile or so in style. But Domenico's spiritual sustenance was strictly rationed. He was allowed into St Illtyd's just twice a year – Christmas and Easter.

In the best photograph that survives of the couple, they stand in their garden four-square to the camera. They are approaching old age and standing between them is a confident, well-fed grandchild. The luxuriantly bearded Domenico, a keen gardener as well as a miner, stands with his left hand firmly planted on the handle of a shovel, a tool with which he seems so familiar it has become an extension of his arm.

The boy and his grandmother wear the look of a people at ease with their identity, firmly rooted in the soil on which they stand. They stare straight into the camera, unafraid of the new technology. But

Domenico has a postured, artificial stance, his left hand tucked uneasily into his side as if he is not sure what else to do with it. The camera holds no interest for him. Instead, his eyes fixed on a far horizon, he remains the exile, part of him forever held by a land and a people a thousand miles away.

He came from a part of the Apennine Mountains in Northern Italy bordered in the south by the great port of Genoa and the fishing town of Chiavari, and in the north by the Renaissance cities of Piacenza and Parma. The mountains between rise to around 6,000ft and are often breathtakingly beautiful, their slopes covered in thick forest, their fields studded with outcrops of brilliant white limestone or black and red quartz. It harbours a rich abundance of plant and wildlife.

But however bounteous Nature has been to these mountains, she is less generous to men. For millennia, peasant farmers have fought to scratch a living out of the unproductive soil. For much of the time they have failed, forced to emigrate to feed their families. Towns like Bardi, Bedonia and Borgotaro stud the north of the area. To the south are the valleys which run inland from the Ligurian coast.

Domenico was born in one of those valleys, which had earlier produced Christopher Columbus's family. A few miles away are the tourist traps of the Italian Riviera. But the poverty in which he was born could not have been further removed from the lifestyle of the rich, like Giuseppe Verdi, born 70 miles from Domenico, who regularly wintered in Genoa's best hotel. Domenico's mother, fighting a losing battle to feed her growing family, set her eldest boy on a path followed by hundreds of others in the area. She bought him a barrel-organ and sent him to London.

Even after he had settled into his new and relatively prosperous Merthyr lifestyle, he never forgot his roots. He and Mary journeyed at least once to Italy to see his brothers and sisters. When other Italians arrived in Merthyr in the late nineteenth century, Domenico became the growing community's elder statesmen, offering them his knowledge of local culture, perhaps teaching them a sentence or two of the Welsh in which he had become fluent.

Among them were those from his part of the Apennines, from towns such as Bardi and Bedonia. Some, like him, became miners. But others, such as the Bernis, destined to revolutionise the eating habits of the British through their Berni Inns, went into catering. They opened the Italian cafés and fish shops which became as characteristic of the Valleys as pubs and chapels and miners' institutes. They included the Basinis.

## DOWLAIS HIGH STREET AND PENYWERN ALFONSO STREET

The cornflower blue and yellow plaque above the grimy door penetrates the gloom of Dowlais High Street like a burst of sunshine. It depicts a carpenter with his saw hard at work at his bench. In front of him a boy working at his own small bench duplicates his father's quiet industry. Above them, the hovering figure of the wife and mother envelopes both with her boundless love. The flowing Middle Eastern robes and the golden haloes surrounding their heads betray their identity. The legend, Sagrada Familia, spells it out – the Holy Family, Jesus, Mary and Joseph.

In a mountain top village in Portugal or Spain its display would be a commonplace of Catholic piety. But here in the heavy, lightless centre of Dowlais it is as unexpected as a howl of flamenco. It is proof of the continuing links between this rainswept hillside in South Wales and the Mediterranean. Those links go beyond the odd Italian street entertainer turned miner, or the cafés that produced me and that once dotted these streets. Names like Hernandez, Estebanez, Cuesta and Perez which still stud the telephone book tell of a Spanish connection that has helped to shape Dowlais and the rest of Merthyr. In Dowlais they once amounted to a colony of almost 2,000 people. It had its own pubs, stores, music. In the colony's streets, Catalan and Galician, the dialects of Aragon and Andalusia, drowned out Welsh and English. Their songs, sung to the inevitable accompaniment of guitars, pipes and accordions, danced through the mean and filthy hovels into which they were herded. Their colour-ful dances mesmerised the natives, like the policeman who, worried that their wild, erotic sardana played on Catalan bagpipes would fatally under-mine Dowlais's nonconformist sobriety, arrived to disperse a group of Spanish dancers one night early in the last century. Intoxicated by the rhythms, he stayed to join in. Dowlais's Spaniards contributed to the town's architecture and its topography.

Predictably, it was the economic power of the ironworks that drew them here. They came from the Basque port of Bilbao and its hinterland. The area had its own tradition of iron-making and a vast store of iron ore. Its relationship with South Wales stretched back into the nineteenth century when dwindling reserves of British ore forced companies like Dowlais to look to Europe for the supplies they needed. Dowlais bought a share in a Spanish mine and began to import hundreds of thousands of tons each year. From the beginning the odd worker accompanied the ore ships determined to find work in Cardiff or Merthyr. But it was not until army recruitment for the Boer War of 1899 to 1902 drained the Dowlais works of men that the company began to recruit Spanish workers on a large scale. They arrived by the dozen, their songs and dances and guitars providing solace for their gut-wrenching homesickness. They came from all over Spain, driven first by their hunger for work to the mines and steelworks of Bilbao before embarking on the great adventure to Dowlais.

The pioneers had left a country mired in poverty where life-expectancy was a mere 35 years. Even so they must have wondered what they had let themselves in for when they arrived in the cold and grime of rainswept Dowlais. Shortage of accommodation in even the meanest Dowlais street meant that some had to cram twelve to a room in local public houses while they began their back-breaking, dangerous work in Dowlais's furnaces and rolling mills. The company tackled the shortage by building them their own street. It is still there, long after most of the Dowlais that once surrounded it has disappeared.

In Penywern, beyond the miraculously preserved Dowlais Stables that housed the works' horses and the town's first school, beyond

Gwyn Alf Williams' plaqued birthplace in Lower Row, down the street where the soldiers who put down the 1831 uprising were barracked, you come to a row of clean, square bungalows rising to barriers that overlook the Heads of the Valleys Road. They resemble those nondescript cottages that seem to grow out of the borders of hair-pin mountain roads in Italy or Spain. Originally, they were starkly simple: two bedrooms, a living room, a small kitchen, an outside loo. Today, adapted for modern living, they are pleasant starter homes for newly-weds, like the young couple with a small baby who were happy to show me theirs. Once, each would have housed a Spanish family of six or more. They would have appeared the height of luxury to those compatriots forced with their families into the slums and cellars of Horse Street or Brecon Street or Erin's Court.

The line of thirteen bungalows was quickly labelled 'Spanish Row'. But its given name is Alphonso Street, after Alfonso XIII, the Spanish king who was on the throne when they were built. His eventful reign reflected a troubled country riven by political violence. An anarchist tried to kill Alfonoso and his wife, Ena, the daughter of the English Edward VII, by throwing a bomb at their carriage on their wedding day. In 1931, Spain voted to become a Republic and Alfonso went into exile. His fate would help to trigger the 1936 Civil War between Republicans on one side and Franco's nationalists and the monarchists on the other.

These days, 'Spanish Row' contains no families with Spanish names, an indication, perhaps, of the success with which the Spaniards integrated. The numbers of Jones or Williamses who now claim Spanish blood in Merthyr is striking. Not that the Welsh always embraced the Spaniards with enthusiasm. Historian Gwyn Alf Williams, the product of an impeccably middle class Welsh family, remembers in his memoir, *Fishers of Men*, his mother's determined opposition when he announced he was going to marry Maria, the daughter of a Dowlais-Spanish family.

For generations the Dowlais-Spanish remained deeply loyal to Spain, however many years they had spent away from the country. For some that loyalty exacted the ultimate price. Ramon Rodriguez, a young ironworker who lived in Market Street, Dowlais, was among the first Welsh volunteers to fight for the Republic against Franco's rebels in the Civil War. He died in the bloody battle of Brunete in 1937, blown up by an artillery shell as his friend, Lance Rogers, also from Merthyr and another hero of the Spanish Civil War, stood next to him in the front line.

"I can see Ramon now," Lance Rogers recalled 60 years later. "I can see the blood that was around the boy. It was terrible, terrible."

Dowlais's Spanish connection is now fading into history, a curiosity in the family history of many in the town and the rest of Merthyr. But its links with Southern Europe still flourish, as that plaque on the house in Dowlais High Street illustrates.

## GWYN

The wind howling through its narrow windows, and the sea thundering on the rocks below, made the west classroom in the tower of the Old College in Aberystwyth the graveyard in which the reputations of generations of lecturers were buried. Having to compete with the wild Cardiganshire coast in their bids to reach students rising in tiers to the distant ceiling reduced most to loud, indecipherable harangues. Others, giving up the unequal struggle to communicate, lapsed into inaudible mumbles.

But for one combative, mercurial ex-soldier the cavernous lecture room became in the early Sixties the launching pad from which he soared first to local fame, then to international stardom. Historian Gwyn Alf Williams, at 5ft 3ins so small he could barely peer above the desk at the front of the lecture room, combined intellectual power and a passion for his subject with a near telepathic ability to connect with his students. He could make even the driest aspects of Welsh medieval land tenure or the structure of the ancient Celtic church as relevant to their lives as Bob Dylan's lyrics. They loved him for it. They flocked in their hundreds to listen to him whatever their subject. A lecture by Gwyn Alf became unmissable.

Despite his size – or perhaps because of it, he was adept at turning potential handicaps into attributes – he was a glamorous figure. He had a matinee idol's looks on top of a boxer's barrel-chested frame. Huge eyes, burning as fiercely as the best South Wales steam coal, dominated the strong face beneath the sweep of dark hair. His experi-

ences fighting as an 18 year-old on bloody Normandy beaches just after D-Day gave a street-wise edge to his fiery left wing radicalism, forged during his childhood in the depressed 1930s. He was dangerously unpredictable, carrying a threat of unruly passion about to spill into anger, which made him irresistible to his students and envied and feared by many of his colleagues. He spent a lifetime moving from political party to political party in a bid to find a home that suited him completely. He failed, but his belief in the ideals embodied by the Russian Revolution and by the fight against Franco's fascism in Spain never wavered.

His birthplace may have been barely 100 miles from the lecture room in which he began to forge his reputation as an historian; but Lower Row, Penywern was a universe away from the patterned elegance of Aberystwyth's Georgian terraces. Today it is an anonymous street whose houses are considerably larger than most workers' cottages. In 1925, the year of his birth, it looked down from its ridge on the clamour and grime of Dowlais with just a suggestion of middle class distaste. Across the road, in a hollow that swept down towards the centre of the town, the clangs, roars and rumbles of the Ivor Works assaulted his ears 24 hours a day. The works, with its forges, furnaces and tall chimneys, was an offshoot of Dowlais's main steelworks which began further down the town and sprawled south for two miles. The Ivor was named after the son of Sir Josiah John Guest, the man largely responsible for making Dowlais synonymous with iron and steel.

When Gwyn was born, the main works with its banks of furnaces, its huge mills rolling out locomotive rails for the world, its hundreds of miles of tramroads and railways, its network of coal mines, still thrived. But within five years it would be closed, killed off by the changing economics of the industry. Only the much smaller Ivor Works survived. Thousands of men were thrown out of work and their families pushed to the edge of starvation. Even in stricken South Wales, Dowlais stood out as a blackspot of deprivation. Unemployment topped 90 per cent. Memories of an earlier working class injustice lapped the young Gwyn's doorstep. Two hundred yards from his front door stood Barrack Row, which had housed the soldiers brought to Merthyr to put down the Uprising of 1831. He would become the undisputed authority on that rising and its martyr, Dic Penderyn.

The politics he learned from the Dowlais of his youth and its history were reinforced by the volumes of the Left Book Club collected by his father. His beliefs focused around the Spanish Civil War and the fight against fascism. But like many champions of the working class, his roots grew in a middle class culture. Both his parents were teachers, his father the headmaster of the Dowlais Central School founded by Sir Josiah John Guest's indomitable wife, Lady Charlotte. His family brimmed with cultural achievement. His uncle, Leyshon Williams, was a well-known playwright, writing regularly for the BBC. The novelist T. Rowland Hughes was another relative. Later, Gwyn would temper the mechanistic, anti-individual, some would say anti-human, politics of his Marxism with the cultural and political nationalism he shared with his hero, the Italian communist Antonio Gramsci.

Religion, too, played its part in shaping him. His family worshipped at the Gwernllwyn Independent Chapel, long since disappeared in the waves of redevelopment that have left Dowlais an urban landscape studded with gaps, like an old man's mouth. Declaiming poetry from the chapel's pulpit helped to shape the dramatic talent he inherited from his uncle and which made him the best after dinner speaker in Wales, as well as a great lecturer and television performer. The stammer he developed merely added to the charm of his delivery. Some suspected he had acquired it deliberately.

My time and his at Aberystwyth overlapped by about 18 months. But, wrapped in a cocoon of depression woven by my mother's terminal illness and teenage angst, I was one of the few to resist his reputation. It would be more than a decade before, as a journalist in Cardiff, I met him to interview him. I discovered the astonishing

range of his intellect and his work: books on the Spanish artist Goya, medieval London, the French Revolution, Madoc the Welsh prince who allegedly discovered America, a shelf-full of volumes on his beloved Gramsci. His brilliant television programmes were object lessons on how to make history vibrantly alive. He pioneered the way for the procession of historians who now fill our screens.

His love for the twin towns of Merthyr and Dowlais was infectious. His masterpiece, *The Merthyr Rising*, an exploration of the riotous year of 1831, helped me to make sense of my town's schizophrenic personality in which a love of culture jostles with a worship of violence, a generosity of spirit battles with a snarling meanness, an outward-looking cosmopolitanism contrasts with small-town self-importance. For all of us who love Merthyr he has become, in that useful phrase diminished into cliché, our remembrancer.

He shared the faults of those of volcanic passion, great warmth and deeply-held beliefs. He had a trigger temper and an elephantine memory for slights, real or imagined. His heroic energy and appetite for work were offset by frequent collapses into depression. I remember calling round to see him for an interview, arranged the day before, to be greeted by a note fixed to the front door saying he was too ill to see anyone.

We met often enough to share a mutual respect; perhaps something more. A few years before he died – at 70 a decade too soon – in 1995, I went with my girlfriend to a party he threw in Cardiff. She watched him greet me with his usual Russian bearhug. "He loves you," she murmured later. I had never thought of it before, but perhaps she was right. Now as I wander down Lower Row into a Dowlais that is a shadow of the vibrant industrial society that produced him, I find myself thinking, "Well, Gwyn, wherever you are, I love you too."

## GLANMOR

Anywhere else in the world the birth of two ground-breaking historians within a half a mile and five years of each other would seem a remarkable coincidence. Here in Dowlais, where history hangs on the air as tangibly as smoke once did from tall ironworks chimneys, it seems as natural as grass growing. Even now, when waves of demolition have wiped away most of the industrial

town, the past still occasionally erupts into the landscape. The Dowlais Works' huge Engine House, for example, that once produced the blast for rows of giant, pot-bellied furnaces has been renovated as a community centre. Its sheer size suggests the scale of what was once the biggest ironworks in the world.

A few breathless yards up the steep High Street the forbidding Guest Memorial Library lowers over the surrounding streets. The gloom of its heavy grey stone is lifted by the delicacy of its cornice and portico. If the elegance of the pillared façade reminds you of a Greek temple, the comparison is intended. It was opened in 1863 as a memorial to Sir Josiah John Guest, the ironmaster largely responsible for Dowlais and its works. Its architect, Sir Charles Berry, the designer of the Palace of Westminster, planned it to resemble the Parthenon, itself an indication of the ambition and wealth of Victorian Dowlais.

Here history lives. Tales of the terrible tragedies and injustices of the past, however remote, are passed on from generation to generation like family heirlooms. So it was that a small boy, with Dumbo ears and an impish smile that would last his long life, learned on his grandfather's knee about the martyrdom of Dic Penderyn, hanged for a crime he did not commit during the Merthyr Rising of 1831. He felt the same heady combination of sorrow, pride and anger experienced by generations of Merthyr children down the years.

When Glanmor Williams was born in 1920, the Guest Library stared gloomily out over a crowded and vibrant Dowlais of 18,000 people. Four thousand men, boys and women poured through gates of the iron and steelworks each day. As members of a community drawn from all over of Europe they were, often still are, acutely aware of their differences. They spend lifetimes climbing into their family trees.

The young Glanmor Williams fell in love with his town's raw, vulnerable humanity. He would spend a lifetime exploring the roots of his family, his community, his country. The same forces worked on the imagination of another hugely gifted child born just five years after Glanmor and within shouting distance of his home. Gwyn Alf Williams, too, learned about the Merthyr Rising from stories told around the family hearth. The two men would trigger a growth in the quality of Welsh historical studies that would make the subject a cornerstone of Welsh culture. Their example produced a succession of gifted young academics who would make history the instrument with which Wales could define its present as well as its past and create a future.

They shared more than a birthplace and a surname. They were physically small men from Welsh-speaking families in which nonconformist religion played an important part. They went to the same grammar school, Cyfarthfa Castle, and the same university, Aberystwyth. Much of their working lives was spent exploring Welsh history. The similarities serve to highlight their differences. Some are suggested by their birthplaces. Lower Row, Penywern, where Gwyn Alf was born, is a terrace of neatly-maintained houses, bigger and more imposing than the mean workers cottages that once surrounded them. From its ridge its residents could look down on Dowlais, socially as well as physically. Glanmor Williams grew up, the son of a miner three times seriously injured, in Francis Street, separated by what was once a busy railway line from Lower Row. It is a tightly-packed terrace of workers' houses that tumbles untidily down a steep slope towards the round, red brick splendour of St Illtyd's Roman Catholic Church. The houses are smaller, more cramped than those in Lower Row.

As we have seen, Gwyn Alf was born into the cultural aristocracy of the Valleys. An uncle was a famous playwright, another relative a

Welsh-language novelist. He was born to achievement and, as the son of a teacher who became a headmaster, to a certain comfort. Glanmor, as his autobiography suggests, had to fight for every rung on the ladder. Research for his doctorate thesis had to be completed in the time he snatched from his teaching job. He had no money to study full-time. The differences also show in their temperaments. Gwyn was emotional, mercurial, his interests as wide-ranging as his talents. He switched effortlessly to writing and presenting memorable television programmes once his career as an academic historian had ended prematurely. Glanmor spent all but two and a half years of his 40-year career teaching at Swansea University. True to his temperament, he focused on one period of Welsh history, the Reformation.

Despite the fact that they were born into the same community and the same generation, they were never close. They circled each other warily, the big beasts of the academic jungle. Glanmor in his autobiography does pay Gwyn a brief but generous tribute. Gwyn was the better writer and perhaps produced the better books. But there are those who would suggest a downside to his brilliance. He wrote too much, too loosely, they argue. And sometimes – perish the thought! – he allowed his left-wing politics to temper his academic impartiality. Glanmor brought meticulous preparation and a warm humanity to his scholarship, even if his good sense and balance are sometimes enough to exasperate the most dedicated fan.

In one area I suspect Gwyn Alf would cheerfully acknowledge the superiority of his fellow historian from the other side of Dowlais's tracks. Glanmor through his warmth and generosity turned the history department at Swansea into the forcing ground for the new generation of Welsh historians. It is remarkable how many of the men and women who populated our history lecture rooms and our television screens in the past forty years passed through his department to study under him or to work with him. They unfailingly remember the help he gave them in shaping their careers. In that sense he may have been the true father of the renaissance in Welsh history which has done so much to shape our national life.

Like the bareknuckle champions who once fought each other to a standstill on the mountains surrounding Merthyr, Glanmor and Gwyn Alf each have their legion of admirers and detractors. For once I am happy to have foot in both camps, grateful for the fact that this small corner of Wales could produce two men of such talent and love for their people.

## OLD ENGINE HOUSE

The two mile journey to work at the Old Engine House in Central Dowlais each day takes Paul Marshallsea to the front-line in a war he has fought for more than a decade. The fact that its weapons are five-a-side football, netball, computer games, dancing lessons and aerobics classes does not diminish its life-and-death urgency.

The enemy are the drug dealers who operate on street corners or in the shadowy recesses of public houses to dole out their pills and powders to the young people of Dowlais and Merthyr.

It is a war that has torn a gaping hole in the heart of Marshallsea, a passionate, inspirational, infuriating man with a street-orator's rhetoric and eyes that burn in rapid turn with pain, laughter and conviction. His youngest son, Stephen, approaching 30, is in Swansea Gaol serving the latest in a series of sentences for violence induced by his drug addiction. "He is a quiet guy, really," murmurs his father, his face contorting with emotion. "But drugs drive him to the point where he does nasty and violent things. They change his personality. He turns into a monster.

"He'll take anything that's going to give him a high. I found him sniffing petrol one day."

At stake in this conflict, he believes, is the future of communities like Dowlais and Merthyr. "Drugs is the only thing which could destroy us from within, like the Romans were destroyed from within by their vices. It is eating us like a cancer. Ninety per cent of the people in jail are there because of drugs."

The war has become a personal crusade. "Every morning now I get up for a fight." And it involves nothing less than the triumph of good over evil. "There is nothing worse than seeing your flesh and blood destroyed from within. My boy was taking drugs and I felt as if Satan was in my front room." At one point, his anger overwhelmed him. "I put my loaded gun – a 12 bore shotgun – in the car and went to shoot the dealers. I knew exactly where they were. I still know where they are."

As he pulled up outside the pub, he reached for the gun in the back of the car. He paused. "I realised I would be destroying my life as well as theirs. And who would be there for Stephen then?"

He returned home and put his gun away. He turned to a lesson rammed home to him by a youth worker in Australia. He was there on an exchange visit as a football referee and a coach. He remembers refereeing at a club for Italian-Australians outside Brisbane. "It was a beautiful place with the very best equipment and a room full of trophies. I talked to the man who drove the club's bus and who knew everything there was to know about it. He pointed to one of the trophies. 'See that cup? It's like a child's life. If you fill it up to the brim with beautiful things, the crap like drugs and alcohol and teenage pregnancy may also get into the cup, but it won't stay there because it is already full with good things. Go home, get yourself a base and give the kids there everything you can, the full package.'"

He has followed the advice to the letter. When he came back to Dowlais he began to cast around for a building in which to fill the lives of Merthyr's youth with good things. He went to see the Old Engine House standing in the centre of Dowlais. Built in 1905, the huge red brick rectangle, more than 50ft high and 174ft long with tall, elegant Georgian windows, housed three massive engines which supplied blasts of hot air to the Dowlais Steelworks' bank of giant furnaces a few yards away.

After the works closed in 1929, the building had gone through a series of reincarnations, including a time as a storage warehouse for the chocolate factory next door. When Paul Marshallsea stood before it in 2001 it was in a sorry state. Much of the roof was missing and all the windows smashed. "But I knew this building had been destined for me".

He set about displaying the flair for wheeler-dealing he had first shown as a coal merchant twenty years before. He found the funding needed to repair the building and to begin developing it as base for the youth clubs he already ran. He created an indoor football pitch which doubles as a court for netball and basketball, and founded the Dowlais and Pant Boys and Girls Youth Club.

Now around 700 young people use the club each week. There is a computer room with a computer-linked projector and a large screen, a collapsible stage and a dance floor. It has a small café and a conference room which can double as a games room for table tennis. There are dance classes, aerobics and music lessons for budding drummers and guitarists. When we spoke in the Engine House, his ambitions for it included a £2m makeover which would add three more floors.

He had already created five permanent jobs and five part-time ones and wanted to create more. But his battles for funding with Merthyr Borough Council had been, he said, long and unproductive. What he wanted most from them was an extension of the building's short lease. "They call me The Terminator in the Civic Centre because of the number of times I've ended meeting and telephone conversations with the words, 'I'll be back'."

For three years funding for his own job came from Coal Regeneration Trust, set up to breathe new life into coalfield communities. When we met the money was about to run out and he had been forced to look elsewhere. He shrugged his shoulders. "The money is useful to pay the bills, but if I have to I will be happy to work for nothing here." He glows with pride when he remembers the Prince of Wales officially opening the project in 2006. But what gives him most pleasure is the conversations with the parents who visit the complex.

He remembers the woman who leaned on the balcony above the pitch watching a group of sixteen year-olds training. "See that boy down there? That's my son. All his friends are dead from drug overdoses."

The seeds of his long war against drugs were sown when his first wife died. "There I was with sons aged nine and five and a wife in a box in the front room and I couldn't boil an egg." On the day of the funeral he remembers struggling to peel potatoes for a family meal, a task had never attempted before. "I took so much off I ended up with a tiny lump of potato and the tears rolled down my cheeks and dropped on to the potato."

The elder son, Phillip, went to live with his grandmother in Troedyrhiw, four miles south of Paul's home in Pant, the village bordering Dowlais. Stephen remained with him. By the time his younger son was 14, the problems with drugs had begun. Stephen has 'died', his father recalls, twice after overdoses. The second time, Stephen remembers travelling down a dark valley towards a bright light he thought represented a public house and comfort. Then his mother stepped out in front of him and said, 'Go back. It is not your turn.' Stephen became free of drugs when he began his latest five-year sentence in Swansea Prison. But he remains psychologically addicted. "It is the only thing he has known since he was fourteen years old," says his father.

When it comes to business or projects like the Engine House, Paul Marshallsea says without a trace of arrogance, "I can't fail, I don't know how to fail. It is not in my vocabulary." But ask him if he thinks he has failed Stephen and his face collapses into tears. He has not given up yet. With part of his sentence still to serve his father, now remarried, has already found Stephen somewhere to live. "I want to have another go at helping to make him free of drugs. I've got a roof for him and a stable background. I'll keep him as close to me as possible. I have a feeling that with all he has gone through, God has chosen him to achieve something big, far bigger than I have managed."

## LADY CHARLOTTE GUEST

The complaint has a twenty-first century ring. "Gentlemen, I have seen during my many years residence in this town (of Merthyr Tydfil), several English families settled among us, who, notwithstanding their various grades of respectable intellect, still could not surmount their national prejudices and unjust animosities; hence, in their imprudence, uncharitableness, and injustice, they have viewed our national habits and our indefeasible attachment to our ancient language with jealous unkindness…."

The speech was made almost 200 years ago and the speaker was a pillar of Merthyr's Welsh intellectual establishment – the poet, scholar and pioneering educator, Taliesin Williams, son of the brilliant writer, forger and founder of the modern national eisteddfod, Edward Williams, better known by his bardic name of Iolo Morganwg.

Taliesin's protest in 1835 is touched with the anger and bitterness of a man who feels his culture, his language, his very being, threatened by a small but powerful foreign ruling caste. He had a case. Merthyr in the early nineteenth century was an overwhelmingly Welsh and Welsh-speaking town. Of the 2003 households with working families in Merthyr in 1851, for example, more than 1800 had heads who were born in Merthyr or who were incomers from other parts of Wales. Only 200, less than one in ten, were headed by those born in England.

But that tenth wielded a power out of all proportion to their numbers. They formed the top strata of society. The ironmasters and their senior managers were predominantly English, as were the shopkeepers, traders and professionals such as doctors and lawyers. They wielded a near-absolute economic power over the working class Welsh and Irish. Often they were contemptuous of the native culture and its language. One manager at the Cyfarthfa Ironworks claimed that Welsh stultified intellectual development and helped to transmit prejudice and bad customs, a bigotry which reverberates in our own time.

But as Taliesin Williams' speech made at an election celebration in 1835 indicated, not every English incomer was contemptuous of, or indifferent to, the majority. He praised one aristocratic English newcomer whose "lofty mind is, from exalted sympathy, attached to our towering hills: she has adopted our costumes – and our language, from the first day that she honoured Merthyr with her residence, has been the object of her successful study; and beyond all, she has visited the widow of the fatherless, and fed the poor and needy."

The object of this paean was the daughter of Abermarle, the Ninth Earl of Lindsay, and the wife of Sir Josiah John Guest, MP for Merthyr – it was his victory Taliesin Williams was celebrating in his speech – owner of the Dowlais Ironworks and probably the most powerful man in Merthyr. Lady Charlotte Guest returned the affection the people of Dowlais and Merthyr lavished on her. Where many newcomers, such as the traveller George Borrow, saw in Merthyr only a vision of a fiery inferno occupied by "throngs of savage-looking people" she saw it as personifying "Dear Wales! How tame every place is after such loveliness and grandeur." Wales would become "my own dear country", so warm and passionate compared to "cold English decorum". She soon viewed the whole of Merthyr as part of her extended family. Her husband was the typical Victorian paterfamilias ruling as a benevolent despot over not just his wife and children but over noisy, clamouring Dowlais and its surrounds. She invariably referred to him as 'Merthyr'.

Her background could not have been more different from her adopted 'family'. She had been brought up in a fine English country house at

Uffington in Lincolnshire. Her father, the elderly earl, died when she was six and her mother married a local clergyman. Charlotte, alienated from her domineering and manic stepfather, became a self-contained, bookish child with an overdeveloped romantic imagination. Her birth entitled her to move in the best English circles. One of her early suitors was the young Benjamin Disraeli, romantic novelist and future Conservative prime minister. She opted instead for marriage to a 'tradesman', a middle-aged, handsome ironmaster who, whatever he may have lacked in social standing, brought with him a hugely successful business – Dowlais would soon be the biggest ironworks in the world – and a massive fortune.

The marriage would be a happy and productive one. Their ten children arrived in quick succession. Dark, fine-boned with huge olive eyes, Charlotte recognised she had been given everything women could wish for – a loving, successful husband, beauty and great wealth. Among her presents on one wedding anniversary were earrings that had been worn by the Empress Josephine. In London she gave lavish balls for Josiah John Guest's political and her society friends. In Dowlais, their imposing home stood in the shadow of the works' massive, smoke-shrouded furnaces. She would walk around the works at night, delighting in the infernal sights which awed and horrified so many visitors. There, too, she entertained lavishly. Her guests included Prussian aristocrats and Russian Grand Dukes – customers of her husband's – the greatest engineer of his day, Isambard Kingdom Brunel, and the mathematician credited with inventing a forerunner of the computer, Charles Babbage.

Intensely curious and driven to fulfil her intellectual potential, she chafed under the restrictions, nineteenth century notions of the dutiful wife and mother imposed on her. She delighted in invading the preserves of the male and she shocked those around her by indulging her love of billiards. In 1840, seven years after her wedding, she complained bitterly that, "I have learned there is but one answer to the question I have so often asked myself, 'What can a woman do?' 'Nothing'!" A more accurate answer in her case would have been "plenty"!

She studied Latin, Persian and Italian. But it was the language and culture of her husband's workforce which fascinated her. She began to study Welsh shortly after she arrived in Dowlais in 1833. She rapidly became confident enough in her new language to attempt a translation of part of the Gospels from Welsh into English. She turned to a collection of medieval Welsh stories she saw as offering her children valuable lessons in chivalry. Several Welsh scholars helped her with her translation of the *Mabinogion*, or "the Mabinogwn" as she called it, into English. Among them were two clergymen, the Rev Tom Jones, bardic name, Tegid, and the Rev Thomas Price, bardic name Carnhuanawc. The translation would earn her a permanent place in Welsh literary history. But perhaps her most important gift to 'her' ironworkers is symbolised by a building which remains an island of beauty in the shabby sea of modern Dowlais.

## DOWLAIS STABLES

The lamps triggered by the onset of dusk this cold March evening extend the 75-metre length of this elegantly-proportioned building. Their soft light highlights the mellow purple warmth of the stone. A squat tower at each end of the façade adds a suggestion of height to its two storeys. The voluptuous curve of an archway, dividing the structure in two, softens sharp lines and right angles. Its sensuality is taken up by the curve of a row of ten small, black-painted windows. A parallel row below remains uncompromisingly square. Above the arch stands a triangular frontpiece which holds a clock with roman numerals. Topping it all is a wooden cupola too slight for the weight of the building. It is the only jarring note of a Georgian edifice whose grace belies its mundane function.

The survival and restoration of the Dowlais Stables, built in 1820, is a miracle in a Merthyr where so much of its epoch-making industrial heritage has been demolished or allowed to decay beyond repair; the Iron Bridge, only the second to be built, which once spanned the Taff and whose remains rotted in the corner of a council yard for years; the unique, early nineteenth century workers' cottages, known as The Triangle, long since bulldozed into history; Joseph Parry's Bethesda Chapel torn down to make way for a road. The list is long and growing.

Down the hill from the Stables, opposite the imposing Edwardian bulk of the Dowlais Library, is St John's Church, in which stands the grave of its benefactor Sir Josiah John Guest. It was built seven years after the Stables, but locked up, its churchyard overgrown and strewn with rubbish, many of its narrow gothic windows broken and boarded up, it looks as I write close to terminal decline.

That the Dowlais Stables, standing on a ridge overlooking the hollow that once contained the ironworks it served, still stands is a result of the hard work of the Merthyr Tydfil Heritage Trust and a local housing association. The disappearance of so much of the Dowlais that hemmed it in emphasises its beauty. The Market Hall, built in 1844, which fronted it, has been demolished, replaced by a small park. The workers cottages flanking it have long gone. Only the brutishly modern concrete and glass tower of a new Anglican church, protruding into view on its north side, mars its symmetry.

The Stables were built by the Dowlais Iron Company to house the horses used to haul trams inside the works less than a mile away. The animals clearly enjoyed better living conditions than many of the workers. But under the paternal rule of Sir Josiah John Guest and later, his remarkable wife, Lady Charlotte, the families of the ironworkers quickly shared its benefits.

Like many of his fellow ironmasters, Sir Josiah John recognised early the role education could play in improving the profit-making skills and efficiency of his workforce. From its beginning the top floor was used as a schoolroom for the sons of ironworkers. A girls' school, using a nearby farmhouse, opened later. Sir Josiah John insisted on employing only qualified teachers. Soon after her marriage in 1833 Lady Charlotte threw herself into the organisation and running of the works' schools. She helped to reshape them into junior and senior sections. Infant schools were added and Lady Charlotte herself began adult classes for the men and women who worked at Dowlais. Anxious to ensure they maintained the highest standards, she toured the growing classes and the multiplying venues with an indefatigable energy, despite her many other commitments which included ten children. She visited schools all over South Wales in search of better methods she could bring to Dowlais. She even took over some of the teaching duties, experimenting with new methods such as using cards and pictures to reinforce the teaching of the scriptures. In the mid 1840's she opened a workingmen's library in Dowlais.

When it became obvious the Stables and other buildings used as schoolrooms could no longer cope with the growing numbers anxious for an education, she pressed her husband to build a purpose-built school. Sir Charles Barry, soon to build the remarkable Guest Memorial Library which stands half a mile up Dowlais Hill from the Stables, was hired to design the new building. The Dowlais Central School opened in 1855, a showpiece for Victorian architecture. It contained a huge central hall with a church-like façade and a massive window studded with gothic arches. The building, demolished in the 1970s, glowered with galleries and flying buttresses. It housed 650 boys and girls and 680 infants.

Sir Josiah John died in 1852, long before the school could be completed. It was the signal for his widow to begin a new era in her life. She successfully took over the running of the works. Then she fell in love with her children's tutor, Charles Schreiber, fourteen years her junior. When they married she began yet another new life, this time as tireless traveller and collector of rare porcelain. She spent most of her time at Cranford near Wimborne in Dorset, the country estate she had bought with Sir Josiah John, or at her London home. Her visits to Dowlais became rarer. But she never lost her affection for its people. It is still reciprocated. Two streets flanking the Stables are named after her. A Dowlais public house called The Lady Charlotte has metamorphosed into a café.

Time has not been kind to her reputation nor that of her first husband. Their insistence on treating the people of the Merthyr and Dowlais as helpless children becomes intolerably paternalistic and smug when viewed against the backcloth of Merthyr's long history of poverty and depression. If Sir Josiah John's unbridled capitalism brought considerable prosperity to Dowlais, his ironworks left it in a desperate economic plight when it all but withdrew from the town in 1930.

Lady Charlotte's feat in learning Welsh well enough to translate the *Mabinogion* into English looks less remarkable to modern critics who emphasise the pivotal role played by the poets and scholars who helped her. In his vivid autobiography, *Unfinished Journey*, the Merthyr novelist Jack Jones gives a revealing insight into the attitudes of her workers to Lady Charlotte and her fellow ironmasters. Jack's grandfather, an out-of-work puddler, an elite ironworker born in 1820, reminisces over the way that, when she ran the company, she implacably faced down Dowlais's striking miners. After a two-month struggle for higher pay they were forced to return to work. "Unconditional surrender was what she had demanded. As bad as old Crawshay himself, she was. Now they were gone, gone to live in their parks at Caversham (the Crawshays' country estate) and Wimborne (the Guests' country home), leaving their old puddlers with constitutions ruined by too much hard work, drinking, and insanitary home life, to fill workhouses and fatten graveyards."

Even at his death in 1852, the affection felt for Sir Josiah John was less than unbounded. When his widow and his colleagues wanted to build the Guest Memorial Library in his memory, they opted to fund it by public subscription. But the money raised fell far short of the £7,000 needed. Instead, the Dowlais Company itself paid for the library and the money raised by the public was used to fund educational scholarships for the ironworkers' children. In our time Sir Josiah John's reputation continues to trigger controversy. When the chain J.D. Wetherspoon wanted to name its new public house in Merthyr after him it triggered local protests. Instead the pub, close to the most important site in the story of the 1831 Merthyr Riots, was named after the miner martyred in those riots, Dic Penderyn.

## CWMRHYDYBEDD

Like the slag tips that smothered its eighteenth century farms, the weight of Merthyr's history as the crucible of the Industrial Revolution in Wales has obliterated much of its remoter past. Popular historians and journalists often reduce the district before the arrival of its four great ironworks to a handful of clichés. They describe a farming community isolated in its mountain fastness which boasted a few hundred lazy yokels. The image is entirely misleading as a glance at sources such as Charles Wilkins' indispensable *History of Merthyr Tydfil* indicates.

The picture that emerges from that and other sources is of a lively and vibrant community with perhaps as many as 4,000 people. As well as hedgers, ditchers and farm labourers, Merthyr and its hinterland boasted an abundance of skilled craftsmen. When the Midlands ironmaster Charles Wood arrived to build Cyfarthfa's first furnace in 1766, he found no shortage of masons, carpenters, sawyers and hauliers, even if some of his stone-cutters were too fond of three-day drinking binges, the postman was an unreliable drunk and his Welsh labourers were half as efficient as their English counterparts.

The fairs in Merthyr and at Twyn-y-Waun on the moorlands above the village were lively days out. Alongside the sale of livestock, stalls offered household goods such as crockery and treats like gingerbread.

Lotteries enabled you to draw tickets entitling you to the best items on a stall. There were sports such as foot races, bareknuckle fighting and 'singlestick', a brutal form of combat involving the use of three-foot wooden staves often made from ash. This poor man's version of the fencers' duel may not have used deadly rapiers, but the staves could inflict crippling injuries. Beer was sold from huge casks and musicians played harps and fiddles. Young farm labourers and servant girls danced, sang, got drunk, flirted and made love.

A lively Welsh language culture thrived in the surrounding farms. Most houses boasted a competent harpist skilled at singing Welsh folk songs. The farms produced an abundance of bards, competing against each other to see who could produce the best impromptu englyn – a four line, often humorous, poem featuring the complex cynghanedd metre. Occasionally, a self-taught but highly skilled philosopher or scientist emerged from an isolated farm, his intellect and his skill earning him a reputation as a magician among his superstitious neighbours.

The domain of elves and fairies was as real as the physical world. Mortals protected themselves against the supernatural by, for example, surrounding a well with a ring of whitewashed stones to keep out the fairies. Gifts of food were placed in fairy rings to win their goodwill. Farmers passed on folk tales to families and friends gathered around their hearths or at inns and fairs. Often they featured ancient heroes such as the twelfth century chieftain Ifor ap Meurig, or Ifor Bach, the ruler of much of upland South Wales, including Merthyr. In 1158, he took on the powerful and treacherous Norman William Fitzcount, Earl of Gloucester, holed up in his castle

at Cardiff, captured him and his wife and held them for ransom. Ifor is said to have had a fortress at Morlais, three miles north of Merthyr in the shadow of the Brecon Beacons. Later it became the site of a Norman castle.

The farmers, craftsmen and small traders formed a vibrant community, passionate in defence of its beliefs and rights. Their fierce pride and willingness to fight for their beliefs made them the true forefathers of the ironworkers and miners soon to forge Wales's first militant working class. The Merthyr of the seventeenth and eighteenth centuries was a stronghold of Dissent, the adherents of Puritanism fighting to follow their religion in the face of a hostile state's punitive laws. Some local families clung to persecuted Roman Catholicism. Politics, like religion, divided families. One brother, for example, was a lieutenant in the Royalist army in the Civil War while his brother held the same rank in Cromwell's New Model Army.

Occasionally industrial Merthyr lifted the corner of a veil to allow us to glimpse this forgotten world. Cwmrhydybedd, the Valley of the Ford of the Grave, was a collection of two dozen houses built on a hillside on the route from Dowlais to Morlais and the Brecon Beacons. It retained much of the atmosphere of a rural hamlet into the twentieth century, despite the fact that it stood in the shadow of the flat-topped slag tip created by waste from the Ivor Works. The Morlais Brook flowed past the houses. It rose in the Bryniau, the high moorland leading to the Beacons which stood two miles above the village, later known simply as The Cwm. South of the hamlet, Gellifaelog Bridge carried the main roads between Dowlais and Penydarren. The bridge gave its name to The Bont, the nearby football pitch which has figured large in the lives of thousands of Merthyr youths and children, including my own.

A revealing article by Gerard Kiley in the *Merthyr Express*, written in the early Seventies, allows us to glimpse life in the little community. One-time Cwm resident, Evan Morgan, born at the turn of the twentieth century, describes a remarkably self-contained and self-sufficient society. Each family grew most of what they ate, tending a vegetable garden and keeping a pig. Trips to Penydarren, two miles and a half penny tram ride away, or to Merthyr a further two miles down the valley, were rare enough to become long-remembered outings. Its self-reliance extended to public morality. When a well-dressed prostitute persisted in coming to the hamlet to tout for trade, The Cwm's matrons took the law into their own hands and dumped her in the fast-flowing brook.

Pre-industrial Merthyr's intense relationship with the world of myth and the supernatural remained vividly alive in The Cwm. The community was intensely aware of the legends which adhered around Morlais Castle perched on a hill on the Bryniau. An early medieval warrior in full protective armour haunted the hamlet. As its name indicated, Cwmrhydybedd may once have been a burial ground for warriors who fought at Morlais. It might even, the people of The Cwm believed, have housed the body of Ifor Bach himself.

Cwm women in particular were prone to encounters with the Devil. One, walking home from nearby Winifred Street in Dowlais, spotted a man standing beneath a gas lamppost. When he began to walk alongside her, she looked down and spotted his cloven hooves. She fled, proving that Beelzebub was no match for the speed of a terrified Merthyr housewife. Another Cwm woman spotted Satan, this time immaculately dressed in top hat, black evening coat and tails. It was an outfit designed to earn any man a devilish reputation in the eyes of nineteenth century Merthyr matrons. Her suspicions were confirmed when she realised he was nine feet tall.

The local authority evicted the people of The Cwm and demolished their houses early 1920s. The land was, for a while, productively cultivated as allotments. Now it is depressingly empty. The Morlais Brook has long since disappeared under successive waves of landscaping. The greening of the famous dirt and cinder football pitch, The Bont, is at least a reminder of the area's rural past. It has at last acquired a thick carpet of grass, largely thanks to the efforts of a local councillor, Clive Barsi. It now boasts nets for its goals and changing rooms. It has become a rare and prized facility for the bored, restless and often violent youth of modern Merthyr.

## VAYNOR CHURCH – THE CRAWSHAYS

It dominates the little country churchyard like a cuckoo in the nest of a tiny and perplexed reed warbler. The horizontal slab of red granite, several yards square in its sheath of iron railings, pushes other tombstones to the graveyard's unkempt corners. Its message, too, in this lovely wooded hollow in a fold of the Brecon Beacons, clamours for attention: 'God Forgive Me'. It is a beyond-the-grave plea you might expect from a monster, a Hitler, a Stalin or at the very least a Jack the Ripper. Instead

the stone, discoloured and partially obscured by its creeping cover of moss and grass, stands over the remains of a man who for decades was seen as their saviour by the thousands who worked for him.

Robert Thompson Crawshay, bald, heavily bearded, with the lugubrious gaze of a bloodhound, was the great-grandson of Richard Crawshay, the arrogant, autocratic founder of the Crawshay dynasty. Under the elder Crawshay's guidance Cyfarthfa Ironworks would became the biggest in Britain. Within thirty years of his death in 1810, it had become the biggest in the world. Richard, a quick-tempered, blunt-speaking Yorkshireman, epitomised the despot industrialist who kept a tight control over the day-to-day running of his company and whose influence over this workforce extended beyond their economic well-being. When I was a pupil at Cyfarthfa Castle, the mock medieval folly built as the Crawshay home which became a grammar school, the legend was that Richard and his successors exercised a *droit de seigneur*, claiming first sexual use of the about-to-be married daughters of their ironworkers. Whatever the truth of that story, the Crawshay males had their choice of the women who worked for them or who belonged to their workmen and they frequently exercised it. The licentious, indolent Francis, half brother to Robert, sired many illegitimate children on local girls, settling a gift of £100 on each child and employing his sons in the family tinplate works he managed at Treforest, 12 miles south of Merthyr, or his daughters as domestic servants. His compliant wife accepted his unorthodox method of recruiting labour without a murmur. But if Francis' indulgence of his overdeveloped libido was accepted as normal by his elders, his brother Henry, industrious and talented, went one unforgivable step further. He fell in love with a local girl and married her. His father, who had regarded him as the most promising of his six sons, ostracised him for so ostentatiously betraying his class. Henry died in charge of a minor Crawshay ironworks in the Forest of Dean, Gloucestershire.

While his father and some of his brothers spent their lives looking after the Crawshays' extensive interests outside Merthyr, Robert lived and died at Cyfarthfa Castle, the family pile which, with its wooded parkland, its boating lake and its carefully cultivated gardens, overlooked the noisy, smoke-wreathed ironworks. During his early years in charge of the works, Robert seemed to embody the best features of Richard Crawshay without his great-grandfather's outsize faults. He loved the works and took a keen interest in its working methods, labouring alongside his men to master their skills. By 1860,

Robert's father, William, who had once been as enthusiastic a supporter of Cyfarthfa as his son, rightly guessed the works was past its productive peak and was against renewing its expensive lease. Robert fought to keep it open and won.

He was a man who prided himself on his reputation as a local benefactor. When the ancient church at Vaynor – nestling below Morlais Castle, three miles north of Merthyr in what is now the Brecon Beacons National Park – threatened to collapse, he paid almost £1,500 to build its small but attractive replacement in the shadow of which his grave now stands. He and his wife, the intelligent, energetic, opinionated Rose Mary, prided themselves on their hospitality. Famous guests at the castle included the American writer Ralph Waldo Emerson, Charles Darwin, the industrialist and philanthropist Robert Owen and the poet Robert Browning. Robert Crawshay was a man of considerable artistic taste. He founded the famous Cyfarthfa Brass Band, the first in Wales and one of the best in Britain with a unique repertoire; Joseph Parry, born in a cottage within the boundaries of the Cyfarthfa works, wrote for it. In 1860 Robert, aged 48, suffered an illness which radically changed his character. A stroke paralysed him and left him profoundly deaf. After what now appears an eccentric, if tasty, course of treatment – his doctors prescribed a large meat chop and two ounces of brandy at frequent intervals, day and night – he recovered his movement. But he remained stone deaf. Isolated and alienated from Rose Mary, he became bitter, resentful and increasingly reliant on the support of his eldest daughter, Rose Hariette, 'Trotty'. To relieve his boredom, he threw himself into a new hobby, the fledgling science of photography.

Having mastered the complex and expensive process, he took hundreds of photographs of himself, his family, servants, brass band and guests. They display a genuine talent for the medium and are invaluable historical documents. The long suffering 'Trotty' posed endlessly for him, often in a variety of exotic and embarrassing costumes. And she acted as his assistant, taking on the primitive and dangerous process of developing the photographs.

But the dutiful daughter was about to prove she had a will of her own. At the late age of 29, after one love affair had been crushed by her jealous father, she fell in love with a Welsh barrister, Arthur Williams. This time she married him despite Robert's implacable opposition. Her father insisted she had promised him she would remain single and look after him until he died. His need for his daughter meant that, despite his sense of betrayal, he remained in touch with her and her husband. But he planned his revenge from beyond that notorious grave. He inserted a clause in his will which stated that after her death her children could not benefit from the £100,000 she had inherited from him.

His treatment of his workers showed the same vindictive bitterness. In 1871, the Government legalised trade unions, a move which was anathema to Robert, a believer in the paternal despotism of his great-grandfather, Richard. When the 1874 recession forced the price of iron to a low point, Robert imposed a swingeing twenty per cent wage cut on his workers. They responded by calling in outside union officials to negotiate for them. Robert's reaction was to begin closing the works, a process completed by March, 1875. It never recovered. Cyfarthfa remained closed until 1879, the year of Robert's death at 62. It opened again, briefly, and was even modernised for steel-making. But after it had passed into the ownership of Guest, Keen and Nettlefolds, proprietors of its great rival, the Dowlais Works, Cyfarthfa closed once more in 1910. It re-opened to meet the demand for steel during World War I, but in 1919 it finally passed into history.

It may have been Robert's remorse at his vengeful treatment of his beloved daughter, or his conduct towards his workers, that prompted the spine-chilling plea on his tombstone. But his behaviour as death approached gave meaning to that macabre appeal for divine forgiveness.

## GURNOS

If the life of the boxer Johnny Owen, brought up on the Swansea Road, was a salute to the heroic best of Merthyr's bleak council estates, a funeral fifteen years after the fight that killed him signified their murderous worst. The funeral, on the same rain-swept mountain where Johnny had been buried, was the climax of a horrific crime that chilled Merthyr's soul even as it riveted its attention. Three weeks earlier, on October 11 1995, a mother and her two young daughters died in a fire at their home at 62 Marigold Close in the north west corner of the vast Gurnos estate. Once the biggest housing project in Europe, its reputation for mean urban violence mocks its rural idyll street names – Magnolia Close, Sycamore Road, Honeysuckle Close, Cherry Way. Diane Jones, a vivacious woman of twenty-one and a fiercely loving mother, was found with her arms around thirteen-month-old Sarah Jane in a desperate attempt to protect her from the smoke and the flames. The fire's other victim was Shauna, named for her father and just two years old.

The police soon established it was no accident. A piece of wood nailed over the lower section of the front door had been prized open and petrol poured into the hall. The trial, almost two years after the event, of two Gurnos women for the family's murder revealed a picture of lives in thrall to drugs and alcohol and spent in casual sex, petty crime and violence. Annette Hewins, one of the accused, spoke after her release of her "pathetic existence.... My life was hectic with drugs, shoplifting, going from house to house gossiping, always out of work." The murders reinforced the town's worst fears about the Gurnos and its other 'sink' estates into which those released from the demolished slums of Dowlais, Riverside and Caedraw had been poured.

I covered the burial of the young family for the *Western Mail*. It was an eye-popping shock to those of us used to the bland proprieties of a 'respectable' funeral. The congregation, overflowing from the recently-built St Aloysius Roman Catholic Church into the surrounding streets, displayed the jagged tensions of a community under siege. Raw emotion spilled across the lawn of the ugly, yellow-brick church along with the hundreds of toys, flowers and tearful tributes. Inside, the priest, the late Father Colin Henneberry, struggled to find words to match the intensity of the occasion. His homily, like everything else in the long service, plunged into bathos in

the presence of the brooding figure who sat, hunched between two uniformed prison officers, in the front pew. On the day he celebrated his twenty-third birthday, Shaun Hibberd, Diane's partner and the father of her two children, had been brought from his cell to attend the funeral. A short, slim, square-shouldered man with the hunted eyes of a cornered animal, he sat, head bowed, the sobs undulating through him. A well-known drug dealer on the estate, he was serving two concurrent sentences in Cardiff Prison: for intent to steal from a local hotel and for threatening to kill a policeman. He had arrived in a green Volvo handcuffed to a uniformed officer, and he remained so throughout the service, even when he stooped to kiss Shauna's tiny white casket; even when, a pall bearer, he escorted Diane to the waiting hearse, and returned to do the same for Shauna.

As Hibberd, still handcuffed to his guard, got out of the hearse to stumble to the waiting grave at Pant Cemetery, just a couple of hundred yards from where my parents lie, a ghetto blaster howled out Patsy Kline's 'Sweet Dreams of You'. The pain-filled dirge about a woman's love for an uncaring man, performed by the troubled country singer who herself died tragically young, had been Diane Jones's favourite. Its ear-splitting drone merely emphasised the still indifference of the surrounding mountains dominated by the Brecon Beacons. At the graveside it was the turn of Michael Jackson's 'You Are Not Alone' to blast across the cemetery. Hibberd beat his chest three times in impotent defiance as he bellowed out the line, "You are always in my heart". Then he cried out a heart-rending "I Love you" followed by the chilling "I'll find the killers". It was a moment that transported you to nineteenth century Merthyr's raucous, crime-

ridden ghettoes of China and Riverside, filled with the town's angry, unrepentant outcasts. If Hibberd's display of raw emotion repelled the disinterested onlooker, it also aroused in us a sliver of envy for its hair-raising abandon.

The judge at the June 1997 trial summed up the image of the Gurnos that emerged from the trial. "Dishonesty, drug-taking and infidelity to your partner or spouse is rife on the new Gurnos, if indeed, not compulsory," he told the jury. It was a picture which then, as now, represented only a fraction of the truth. The verdicts of the judge's court were soon discredited. The main defendants, Donna Clarke and Annette Hewins, emerged as victims of a miscarriage of justice. Cleared of murder, they had been convicted of arson with intent to endanger life. They had been given long sentences, 20 years for Clarke, 13 for Hewins. Both convictions were quashed.

For every one Gurnos family living the life graphically described by Annette Hewins, a hundred struggled to bring their children up to live decent, fulfilling lives, often against daunting odds of poverty, unemployment and poor health. Sometimes they succeeded brilliantly. The novelist and teacher Des Barry was brought up on the estate. He went to university and travelled the world looking for a personal fulfilment in his religious and creative life. He has returned to South Wales, teaching young people on the Gurnos creative writing and helping them to achieve their potential.

Even before the horrific murders a concerted campaign by local authorities and charities was underway to improve life on the bleak, sprawling estate which had been built with too few of even the most basic facilities. The Welsh Assembly has since joined in the quest. A bewildering variety of help and advice centres, courses and classes are now available. Their targets range from toddlers to their grandparents. The image and prestige of Johnny Owen has been recruited to the cause. The building which once housed the much-vandalised Matchstick Man public house, named in Johnny's honour, has been converted into the Johnny Owen Centre. It contains, among other things, a housing advice office.

Vandalised corners of the estate – only fifty years old, I remember walking to school past a Gurnos that was still farmland – have been demolished and redeveloped. The house in which Diane Jones died has, along with the rest of Marigold Close, been pulled down and replaced by a series of bungalows for the disabled which boast nothing more menacing than a garden ornament shaped like a ship's

canon. Merthyr Borough Council has begun to refurbish a decaying shopping centre on the estate and a series of flats there empty for almost a decade.

It would be equally myopic to dismiss the judge's comments as mere fantasy. Des Barry, best-known for his novel, *The Chivalry of Crime*, based on the life of the American outlaw Jesse James, describes the Gurnos as "my Wild West".

When he was growing up there, fights spilled on to the streets most weekends. The weapons were often more lethal than fists. A friend was shot and killed in a fight with a neighbour. Another died in a police chase after he had stolen a motor cycle. Barry's second novel, *A Bloody Good Friday*, set in Merthyr, is an epic prose poem set to the rhythms of the street violence he grew up with.

Visit the Gurnos today and the efforts to improve life there are obvious. Proud owners of former council houses have added their own bright ornamentation. Classical vases, nymphs and gnomes adorn lawns. Lantern lamps illuminate front doors. Vibrant murals brighten community help and recreation centres. Shopping precincts have been spruced up. But the signs of a community still under siege from violence and vandalism are everywhere. The wall of a fenced-off playground is decorated with vivid murals of happy local children. But the twenty foot high wire mesh fence above has been painted with black anti-climbing paint. The windows of the Johnny Owen Centre are covered with thick mesh grilles. A nearby community centre has heavy steel window shutters and a steel door thick enough to protect a bank vault.

The Gurnos stands to remind us of the folly and the injustice of herding thousands of people burdened with the same crippling problems of poverty and unemployment and pouring them into identical concrete boxes on vast concrete estates with too few shops or public houses or opportunities for recreation and improvement.

## BWLCH BRECONSHIRE, BUCKLAND HALL

From the road above, the ponderous red sandstone country house, with its castellated *porte-cochere* and huge bay windows, peeps out from its curtain of trees, a likely location for a Harry Potter fantasy or a mannered Jane Austen comedy. Beyond the flame-like bushes and the terraced lawns that front the house, the narrow ledge on which it stands falls sheer away to the River Usk, a stream now, burbling weakly through its rock-strewn canyon. The ridge rising from the far bank is pastured and clustered with trees. White farmhouses dab its emerald green. To the left of the house the bald summit of the 1500ft Tor-y-Foel, an outrider of the Brecon Beacons, is turbaned in wet cloud.

The spot on the road between Brecon and Abergavenny is ancient with history. Through the lush Usk Valley have ridden invaders from the Romans to Henry IV in pursuit of Owain Glyndwr. Dafydd Gam, the fifteenth century warlord who claimed descent from the Welsh princes but who fought for Henry against his countrymen and who later died fighting alongside Henry's son at Agincourt, lived here. A succession of houses has occupied the spot. The latest, Buckland Hall, built of stone from the wooded hill into which it nestles, has the architectural stamp of the Tudor period. But its heavy presence and fussy ostentation marks it as a late Victorian fiction. It was built in the 1890s to replace a Georgian predecessor destroyed by fire. Today it is enterprisingly run as a conference and retreat centre for those interested in holistic medicine, spiritual exercise and alternative culture.

Buckland Hall may lack the power of Cyfarthfa Castle, the refinement of what was Cyfarthfa's Georgian neighbour, Penydarren House, or the artistic flair of William Burges's Cardiff Castle; but in 1919 it was a flamboyant expression of a newly-minted millionaire's wealth and status. Along with the house came a 2,500 acre estate of gardens, parks, farms and a three and a half mile stretch of river full of salmon. The man who purchased it in the year after the end of World War I was a straight-backed, well-groomed businessman and

industrialist, Seymour Berry. He had made the ten-mile trek across the southern spur of the Beacons from his birthplace, Merthyr Tydfil, whose population had just peaked at 80,000. The raucous, lively, licentious town was a world away from Buckland's chatter of birdsong, gently lowing cattle and the hiss of a salmon line cast upon the river. Seymour, forty-three when he bought the Buckland Estate, had helped his father

John Matthias Berry, a former Mayor of Merthyr and the founder of the town's Liberal Club, build the family's estate agency into the biggest in South Wales. The ambitious son had soon branched out into the property business, collecting the rents from his newly-acquired houses himself. His father, known to his offspring – and his wife – as JMB, was, like almost every-body else in Merthyr, an

immigrant. He had been born in Pembrokeshire and arrived in Merthyr as a humble railway employee. He became the constituency agent for Merthyr's Liberal MP, D.A. Thomas, later Lord Rhondda, a member of Lloyd George's cabinet and head of the huge conglom-eration of coal mines, the Cambrian Combine. It may have been JMB's influence that helped Seymour to get a job as secretary to the MP, but the way the son used his position to build up a massive portfolio of shares and directorships in coal and steel owed most to his personal drive and ambition. He is said to have been a director of over seventy-five companies, more than anyone else in Britain.

The drive to success was a family trait, evident in the ice-cold determination in JMB's eyes in the portrait painted by Rolf Harris's grandfather, George Frederick Harris, which now hangs in the Cyfarthfa Museum. Seymour could be said to be the least ambitious of JMB's three sons. Both William (born 1879) and Gomer (born 1883) found Merthyr too small a stage. William, a journalist and Gomer, who worked as a shop assistant in a Merthyr store, went to London where in partnership they established a chain of sporting and trade magazines. It was the foundation for the creation of one of the world's biggest newspaper empires. They owned influential dailies like the *Daily Telegraph* and the *Financial Times*, powerful Sundays such as the *Sunday Times* and forerunners of today's tabloids like the *Daily Sketch* and the *Daily Graphic*. They also had a stable of 'regional' newspapers which included the *Western Mail*. Both became peers, William as Viscount Camrose, Gomer as Viscount Kemsley. Both relished their status as powerful newspaper barons. Among Camrose's close friends was Winston Churchill. Kemsley's intimates

included Ian Fleming, the creator of James Bond. When the brothers split amicably in 1937, Camrose took the *Daily Telegraph* and the *Financial Times*, Kemsley the *Sunday Times*, four other London titles, the *Western Mail* and a clutch of regional newspapers.

But Seymour was far from the hick elder brother, content to mind the family store while his brothers cut a dazzling swathe through the ranks of the powerful. He played an elder brother's role in helping them to finance their business growth and in making crucial decisions. After the purchase of the Buckland estate he was not content to settle for the easeful life of a country gentleman. He, too, had powerful friends. Among the guests at Buckland Hall was Lloyd George. Even today, gossip on the estate describes him as a hard taskmaster. He is said to have liveried his army of servants in vivid red, not as an expression of personal vanity but because their brilliant uniforms helped him to keep track of them and to ensure they were not shirking.

This image of him rings true, but it runs alongside his reputation as a philanthropist who was particularly generous to his home town. He gave Merthyr at least £100,000 and supported a bewildering variety of local causes. Among them was the establishment and growth of the desperately needed General Hospital. His statue, erected by a grateful town outside the hospital, now stands before Merthyr's impressive Central Library.

The act that triumphantly sealed his career, the purchase of the Buckland Estate, also signalled his tragic end. Seymour liked to maintain his middleweight boxer's figure with a pre-breakfast horse ride around a field half a mile from the house. Not a man to waste time on mere recreation, he would order his groom to follow on horseback. That way, he could shout instructions over his shoulder. One morning in May, 1928, Seymour, turning to talk to his servant, did not notice he was galloping dangerously close to a telegraph pole. The groom's warning came too late. Seymour's horse, about to collide with it, shied, sending its rider over its head and into the pole. Seymour's skull shattered. He died instantly. He was not yet fifty-one.

Poles still march through the massive, gently-sloping field, now lush with pasture in which the accident is said to have happened. Thousands lined the streets as his coffin passed through Merthyr on May 26, 1928.

It was not the only tragedy to counterbalance what some might see as the Berry family's excessive good fortune. On October 12 1984, Sir Anthony Berry, sixth and youngest son of Gomer Berry, Viscount Kemsley, and MP for Enfield, as well as a junior minister in Margaret Thatcher's government, was killed when an IRA bomb ripped through the Grand Hotel in Brighton.

## ST ILLTYD'S CHURCH, DOWLAIS

Like a great European cathedral, the smug splendour of St Illtyd's Roman Catholic Church, on its hill on the border between Dowlais and Penydarren, reflects the ambition of those who built it. But their vision was an earthier one than the heavenward search for spiritual fulfilment symbolised by the soaring spires and flying buttresses of the medieval masons. The round, fat-bellied tower that holds St Illtyd's altar and chancel suggests the replete satisfaction that comes with a good meal and the assurance of many more. As you approach its heavy beauty, or sit within its dark, womb-like peace, you sense it was the prospect of a paradise free from grinding poverty and the gnawing anxiety of hunger that galvanised the Irish labourers who built it red brick by red brick.

Walk inside and the self-satisfied Victorian exterior gives way to a riot of baroque decoration matching anything you will find in those great churches which dominate hill-top villages in Italy or Spain. Polished marble pillars support elegant arches. Saints staring out stonily from their plinths guard each side of the entrance to the altar, their heads framed by miniature gothic arches. A marbled red and cream pulpit grows from the wall to the left of the altar, a challenge to any priest to match his words to its opulence. Above the pulpit stands a richly carved Station of the Cross, one of twelve celebrating – relishing – Christ's tortured journey to Calvary.

The sheer size of the interior suggests the yearning for breathing space of a people living cheek-by-jowl in cramped hovels. And here, at last, their search for a life beyond their present veil of tears is symbolised by the white marble altarpiece spiralling into the domed ceiling. It is a daydream of mini-towers, carved clusters of leaves as delicate as lace and spirals of marble, as thin as twists of candy, thrusting for the secrets of heaven. Angels with wings folded and hands closed in prayer lurk within its folds. A figure of Christ in Majesty stands triumphantly at its summit. If the stained glass figures of St Illtyd, St David, St Patrick and St Benedict that flank it are self-consciously traditional, the altar threatens to out-Gaudi the great twentieth century Catalan architect in its romantic flamboyance.

At least that is the way the church looked when I began worshipping there almost sixty years ago, myself and my brother separated by the formidable figure of my mother to prevent us from fighting all over the pew. It was like that when, as an altar boy I took part in the great rituals of Christmas and Easter that packed its pews. It was like that when, as a pupil at St Illtyd's School close by, I was called from the soccer field or the cricket pitch, cursing beneath my breath, to serve mass for the parish priest Canon James, a remote, aristocratic figure who smelt of bitter disappointment. He would have been more at home sipping sherry in a cathedral presbytery or a Vatican sitting room than ministering to a poverty stricken working class community. His frailty was, I suspected, due more to his alcoholism than to an organic illness. He was rarely up before 11 am to say his daily mass.

Today, the Church's move away from liturgical pomp to a simpler ceremony has changed the interior. Much of the baroque decoration has gone, including the stone saints flanking the altar and the splendid pulpit. But the soaring altarpiece and the stained glass windows remain to conjure up an image of the church as it once looked.

The construction of the first St Illtyd's, opened in 1846, was a triumph of personal dedication over hostile circumstance. For decades

at the beginning of the nineteenth century, the Catholic hierarchy looked for ways to cater for the spiritual needs of the Irish who, even before the flood of immigration triggered by the famine, had arrived in numbers to work in the expanding industries of South Wales. Poverty, hardship, the indifference of their flock and the sheer size of the parish often conspired to defeat those priests who to took up the challenge. In 1827, the Irishman Father Patrick Portal became the first Merthyr-based Catholic priest since before the Reformation. He left four years later, his health broken, complaining of "nothing but hardships out and solitude at home". By 1835 he had been replaced by a man who gave the parish its soul as well as its first church.

Father James Carroll was a Dubliner, a classical scholar and a linguist with an MA degree who spoke Latin as fluently as he did English. A short, round man who smelled of the whiskey he was fond of, he insisted on sharing the poverty of his flock. He was a byword for giving away his meagre income to those he felt needed it more than he did. He converted the front room of his tiny house into a shop from which he eked out a living, selling salt fish and the vegetables he grew in his garden. He said Sunday mass in Merthyr in a dank room with holes in its roof, above a slaughterhouse. Then he walked the six miles to Rhymney to say another in a hired wash-house. He established a school in a "one horse stable about 8ft wide and 16ft long" and taught fifty poor children there. A visitor in 1840 described his home as "without a stick of decent furniture" and doubted whether he ever had enough to eat. A witness who spotted him trekking over a bleak mountain to see an ill parishioner noted, you could see his feet though the gaps in his boots.

He moved to Dowlais and single-handedly raised the money for the construction of St Illtyd's, cajoling funds out of Wales's wealthy traditional Catholic families and out of the few Merthyr Irishmen who had clawed their way into the middle class. When he had raised the money he needed, he bought four labourers' cottages on a hill overlooking part of the Dowlais Works, demolished them and began building his church. His parishioners supplied the labour, usually after having spent twelve or fourteen hours a day, six days a week, in the ironmasters' works and mines. Even then his difficulties were not over. The fledgling building is said to have been attacked and flattened several times by its hostile Protestant neighbours. Father Carroll's death symbolised his life. In 1847 he worked tirelessly ministering to the victims of an outbreak of typhus, labelled 'the Irish fever' because of its prevalence among immigrants like his parishioners. It was endemic in Merthyr. He contracted the disease and died just a year after his church opened.

Later the Benedictine Friars arrived and, using the descendents of the labourers who had constructed the original building, they created the lavish church I grew up with and still love. But however impressive the building they created, the soul of St Illtyd's resides in the spirit of a learned Irishman who, Christ-like, sacrificed himself for the poor and downtrodden whose travails he shared.

## DOWLAIS IRISH

When, in the infants school tucked behind the imposing St Illtyd's Catholic Church in Dowlais in the late 1940's, the teacher asked her class of four-year-old Hennessys, Duggans, Murphys, Morans and O'Learys to put their hands up if they were Irish the only one to respond was a chubby little boy whose full name was Mario Patriarco Domenico Giuseppe Bartolomeo Basini. Six years later the boy, having moved 200 yards to St Illtyd's Primary and Secondary Modern School, would find himself singing 'The Dear Little, Sweet Little Shamrock of Ireland' with half a dozen fellow pupils as part of the St Patrick's Day concert. At the appropriate moment he would flourish the huge, luridly green cardboard cut-out of the Irish national symbol he had been hiding behind his back.

To be Catholic in Merthyr and Dowlas was to be Irish wherever you or your parents were born. As an Italian who spoke the language with his mother at home a mile away in Penydarren, my life was dominated by the Irish. At St Illtyd's school I was taught my multiplication tables by Mr Molony, a tall, skeletal southern Irishman with a dark Celtic temperament and a scowl so forbidding it made R.S. Thomas' glower look like a smile. I was a favourite since I was a source of the pipe tobacco he was addicted to. He was forever sending me home to get him another tin from my family café. All the teachers were either Irish or of recent Irish descent. The same applied to the girls' school and the infants nestling behind the fat, round-towered church which stood on a hill dominating the collection of makeshift sheds in which the boys were herded. And the vast majority of the priests I served as an altar boy in St Illtyd's were Irish. There we worshipped to the relentless rhythms of the Irish Catholic imagination, with its emphasis on blood and sacrifice, its insistence on unbending obedience to the rules of confession, communion and fasting.

The religion of the Merthyr Irish reflected their cruel history. In that sense my adopted Irishness mixed easily with my Italian blood. The Italians, too, endlessly oppressed and insulted, were enthralled by the notion of suffering redeemed by acceptance and the promise of eternal salvation. They, too, were in love with images of bleeding martyrs riddled with sword thrusts; of Christ, his Sacred Heart exposed, his cruelly-pierced hands raised in benediction, his bloody head crowned with a twist of thorns.

What cemented my sense of Irishness was the fact that I had been born on St Patrick's Day and had been named after the saint. (The relatives who named me believed that 'Patriarco' translated 'Patrick' into Italian. I should have been called 'Patrizio'). Because we observed St Patrick rather than St David, March 17 was a holiday. I was for any nationality that gave me a day off on my birthday.

The Irish in Merthyr and Dowlais were by far the biggest immigrant group (except for the Welsh themselves). If most had come after the great famine of the 1840s, there had been a strong presence here before then, drawn by the high wages paid in the ironworks and the cheap cost of sea travel. By 1851, there were 3051 Irish-born citizens in Merthyr and Dowlas, 6.6 per cent of the population. In a few years, their population swollen by descendants, the percentage would be much higher. Their numbers made them feared and despised by the Welsh, who believed the Irish were taking the bread out of their mouths by undercutting their wages and steal-ing their jobs. Herded into slums bordering Dowlais High Street, which were impossible to keep clean, they were castigated for being dirty. The *Cardiff and Merthyr Guardian* in 1850 contemptuously commented: "the low Irish are a remarkably dirty race", while "nothing can exceed the cleanliness of the Welshman's cottage or the commendable desire of the Welsh matron to have everything orderly". The managers of ironworks regularly declared the Irish were too stupid and unruly to do any job more skilled than labouring.

The quarrels between the Welsh and Irish had the reckless violence of families at war. The historian Glanmor Williams, in his autobiogra-phy, indicates the derision the 'respectable' Welsh displayed for the Irish they labelled 'Paddies' or 'Plant Mari', Mary's Children. Differences of language as well as religion divided the two communi-ties. Occasionally, their resentments exploded into full-blown riots. On a Saturday night in July, 1850 , for example, the tensions between the newly-arrived Irish and the resentful Welsh erupted into a street fight close to Dowlais's Irish Row. It ended in a Welsh victory. The follow-ing day, the Irish, thirsting for revenge, broke the windows of a nearby Welsh Independent chapel. The outraged Welsh gathered in the streets 1,000 strong. They attacked nearby Irish homes, breaking windows and injuring some. Six people, three Welsh and three Irish, were carted off to the police cells. The fighting continued until the mob turned on the hapless police, bombarding them with huge stones. When order was eventually restored, the riot had lasted three days.

The embers of such clashes still glowed in Dowlais a century later. About half a mile from St Illtyd's School was Gellifaelog Secondary Modern, Welsh and Protestant. It stood on a grassed-over rubbish tip. At regular intervals, when I was at St Illtyd's, fighting broke out between the two schools involving scores, sometimes hundreds of boys. Sometimes the Gellifaelog mob would flood down their slope to charge the boys defending our gates. Sometimes we would rush screaming up the hill to attack them. They were childish re-creations of the storms of the previous century. Nobody, as far as I remember, was seriously injured. But those swarms of howling schoolboys were graphic reminders of the passionate hatreds that once fuelled the relationship between the Welsh and the Irish.

## THE BONT

A patch of reclaimed wasteland hemmed in by the mountainous tips of the Dowlais and Penydarren Ironworks, The Bont bore no resemblance to the great cathedrals of football such as Glasgow's Parkhead or Ibrox. A single blade of grass refused to grow on its dirt-and-cinder pitch. It had more ridges and hollows than the surrounding mountains. Fifty men and a dog crowding the touchline constituted a good crowd. In the summer, its rusting, netless goalposts were taken down to turn it into a cricket pitch on which batsmen, sharing two pads and a splintered bat, thrashed out a game Lords would have struggled to recognise as the bastard son of its bucolic public school pastime. And yet its football matches often generated the same sectarian passion that consumed the clashes between Glasgow's Celtic and Rangers. The Bont became the battleground on which some of the great religious and tribal conflicts of Merthyr were fought.

It was the no-man's land between the armies of Irish

Catholic Dowlais and the nonconformist Welsh. Both the staunchly Protestant Dowlais United – known as The Bont – and the Catholic St Illtyd's, still known contemptuously as 'The Paddies' or 'Plant Mari', regarded The Bont as their home pitch. Their national and religious differences were compounded by their economic rivalry, the Welsh complaining bitterly that the Irish took away their jobs, the Irish protesting at the menial work and low wages they were forced to accept. The matches between The Bont and St Illtyd's, when the crowds swelled to hundreds, frequently degenerated into the sort of mini war that for generations had erupted onto the streets of Dowlais. But they helped to bring a little order to those conflicts and to contain them.

The Bont, within 200 yards of St Illtyd's Catholic Church and its boys school, was my pitch for football and cricket until I was eleven and left for the grammar school. I played in goal for the school's highly-successful junior soccer side which won the north Merthyr championship and, one memorable Saturday morning, played our southern rivals, Troedyrhiw, for the overall title on the vast and properly grassed Penydarren Park, home of Merthyr Tydfil, the best non-league football club in Britain. As a cricketer, too, I liked present-ing the last line of defence. I loved playing wicketkeeper, armed with a pair of ancient leather gloves falling apart at the seams. On The Bont's frontline my job of stopping the balls missed by the batsmen was a dangerous vocation. Catching a hard ball rearing off one of its ridges was like trying to disarm a grenade before it took your head off. Later I rationalised my choice of sporting roles with typical psychobabble. I told myself I had the sort of personality which enjoyed shouldering responsibility, of being the one on whom the rest of the team depended. There is simpler explanation – laziness. As a goalkeeper or a wicketkeeper you don't need to run much.

Even as members of the school's junior football team, we had deep cultural divisions to cope with. We played a team from the village of Heolgerrig on the lower slopes of Aberdare Mountain on the far side of the valley, beyond the metropolis of Merthyr. Travelling to meet them on their mountainside pitch was as disorientating as a trek into the Himalayas. When they played us on The Bont we felt we were under siege by a foreign army. Their players jabbered among themselves in a language that was entirely alien to me. Their teachers howled instructions in the same indecipherable gabble. I felt person-ally intimidated, perhaps a reflection of what my friends felt listening to my mother talking to me in Italian. If they did, they were too polite or too fond of her steaming plates of pasta to mention it. It would take the broadening experience of grammar school to teach me what that foreign language used by our Bont opponents was. It was Welsh.

## THE BONT BOXES

In sport, as in everything, the fiercely independent communities making up the Merthyr Borough like to assert their individuality. While the surrounding valleys succumbed to rugby union, the game invented by an English public school, they united behind the working man's football. In the depressed 1920s and 1930s, Third Division Merthyr Town commanded their loyalties and lifted their spirits. Black-faced miners, fresh from their shifts, poured from their trains on to the terraces of Penydarren Park to cheer them. After the war, the newly-formed Merthyr Tydfil regularly attracted crowds of 10,000. When rugby briefly challenged soccer's supremacy it was in the form of the professional Northern Union, the forerunner of union's deadliest rival, rugby league.

But the sport which encapsulates the town's psyche is boxing and its ancestor, bare-knuckle mountain fighting. Boxing's combination of fierce individual challenge, soul-baring bravery, quixotic chivalry and controlled savagery is the near-perfect expression of the Merthyr's personality. The commitment of some to Merthyr's ideal of physical courage literally cost them their lives. It is no accident that in a town that has produced so many world-shaping industrialists, pioneering politicians, newspaper barons, scientists, artists, composers, novelists and poets, the most recent statues celebrating its heroes have all been of boxers – the great Eddie Thomas, Howard Winstone, and the tragic Johnny Owen whose courage, too great for his frail physique, killed him. It was impossible to grow up in the town and escape fighting: not just the confused confrontations of the school playground, full of sound and fury and flailing haymakers, but encounters with boys of skill and precision for whom the well-made punch was as much an expression of pride in their talent as the carefully-crafted sentence is for the writer.

My nemesis as a fighter came in the shape of a lad, smaller but several years older than me, who rejoiced in the name of Errol Flynn. There was nothing of the swashbuckler about Errol. He was wiry and dark, as taciturn as his handsome Hollywood namesake was flamboyant and verbose. But he fought with an intensity against which the celluloid hero would have quickly crumpled. Errol, too, went to St Illtyd's School. I suspect he had watched me come to the rescue of a friend who was being pummelled in a fight in the school yard and decided that I was worthy of his challenge. He intercepted me as I was walking home for dinner across The Bont, the dirt and cinder football field which stood just south of the school. I took a drubbing. We met the next day and the next. Each time I was as well-beaten as the first. I barely landed a punch on an opponent who fought with a precise, controlled savagery that would later make him, however briefly, a professional boxer. As always in these cases, the physical pain mattered nothing compared to the hurt to my eleven year-old ego.

After a week of these humiliations, my frustration mounting day-by-day, I decided to tell my mother. I mumbled out the story of my repeated beatings, further humiliated by my need to seek her sympathy. Her laugh told me this was one problem I would have to solve myself. I wish I could say that in true Hollywood fashion I found a resolution by eventually thrashing my tormentor, restoring my pride and giving myself a satisfying revenge. My solution was more expedient. I found another way home.

## DOWLAIS IRONWORKS

My parents had the immigrants' faith in the power of education to transform the lives of their children. And my father nurtured a peasant's reverence for those who claimed the skills he never had the chance to acquire, however far-fetched those claims may have been.

He was forever beguiled by the washing machine salesmen, the car mechanics, carpenters and builders he met leaning on the bars of his favourite locals. The washing machine he acquired turned out to be stolen and the ice-cream vans he had manufactured out of clapped out delivery vehicles became, in his own graphic phrase, "a box of bombs." An army of self-styled painters and decorators besieged him, often turning the café into a building site. For decades afterwards I came across men who had once painted it. When as a journalist I went to interview the Falklands war veteran, the cruelly burned and courageous Simon Weston, at his home in Nelson in the next valley from Merthyr, his grandfather told me that he, too, had once been employed by my father to give the café a new look, a process that seems to have been as continuous as the painting of the Forth Bridge.

The stockroom below the shop was filled with the debris of past makeovers. Broken chairs and tables, torn-out and abandoned partitions, tin trunks full of old curtains made the room an Aladdin's Cave for my best friend Mansel Aylward and me. An old bench that protruded from behind some partitions stacked against a wall became, with the aid of a lump or two of modelling clay and a child's imagination, a stage on which we could perform the plays we created. Wrapped in old curtains we became Roman emperors while Carol Fuller, who lived opposite, became our complaining slave. Later a pop bottle suspended on string became the thurible – the Roman Catholic incense-burner – used while I acted out my brief but intense urge to become a priest.

Given my father's desire to help me through school and to hang on every word of those 'experts' he met in the bar of the Crystal Palace or The Talbot, it was inevitable that he found me a tutor to guide me through the eleven plus. Jack Goggin was a spare, thinly pleasant man whose Irish surname said he was as much a part of Merthyr's melting pot as I was. His brief, in the few lessons we had together, was to teach me arithmetic. As we both quickly recognised, I knew as much about the mysteries of multiplication and long division as he did. Instead, he gave me something far more precious than help with an exam I would have passed anyway. He began to teach me about the rich history of my town.

He told me about the four great ironworks that had forged Merthyr. Two of these had been on my doorstep. He told me of the iron and coal mines, the tramways, Trevithick's epic journey

which ushered in the railway age. He described the cataclysmic conflicts between the ironmasters and their employers, the great musicians and politicians. Sometimes he would illustrate his lessons with field trips. The magical day he took me on a journey through the ruins of the Dowlais Ironworks – for decades the greatest in the world – and into history remains indelibly on my memory. The works, which with its railways had radiated for miles from the centre of Dowlais, had closed twenty years before. But much remained to recreate its size and complexity and the sense of danger and excitement it triggered in those who saw it.

We walked to the century-old slag heaps half a mile from my home, which signalled the southern border of the works, and followed its ruins for two miles into its once vibrant heart, a giant bowl scooped out of the surrounding hills. We walked past the ghosts of famous rolling mills which poured out the rails of railways crossing five continents. The tall chimneys of the brickworks still dominated its squat kilns and sheds. The imposing, ivy-clad Dowlais House, home of the Guests who ruled this industrial empire, still stood a few yards from the rusting remains of the huge blast furnaces. Its position, within the walls of the works, testified to the dynasty's determination to share the grime, the clamour and the smoke, if not the poverty, endured by its workers. But the ruins themselves – crumbling walls, abandoned bridges, the decaying skeletons of mills and furnaces – were the main triggers of a child's imagination, as suggestive as the towers and buttresses of a great medieval castle. Jack Goggin revealed a single rail hidden beneath the long grass, still bearing its proud stamp, Made in Dowlais, once as safe a guarantee of quality as Rolls Royce's Silver Lady.

Churning out hundreds of thousands of these rails each year was the mainstay of Dowlais's profitable business for more than century. Its rails snaked across the icy wastes of Siberia. They webbed the prairies and the arid deserts of America, climbed the Rockies and linked the Atlantic and the Pacific. They fuelled the prosperity of Victorian Britain by opening up the vast British Empire in Africa and Asia to economic development. History on this scale justifies Merthyr's often overpowering sense of self-importance.

Now every trace of the ironworks has disappeared, except for the huge engine house that once provided the blast for banks of giant furnaces. The stark slag heaps that encircled the works remain, much reduced and humanised, genteelly grassed over. Part of the great natural bowl once filled by the ironworks is now a private housing estate cloned out of a single red-brick box. South of that is an industrial estate. Where once the ceaselessly working mills poured out the railways that crossed continents, rows of monotonously white, neatly landscaped factories manufacture spare parts for your car, assemble office furniture, print glossy magazines or make Marks and Spencer chocolates. The empty units and unfinished factories belie the optimism of its name, the Phoenix Business Park. The estate is an uncomfortable reminder of Merthyr's much reduced status as it searches with a touch of desperation for a new economic role.

But we remain proudly aware of the time when Dowlais was at the heart of the industrial world, when our ancestors played a crucial role in the creation of the modern world. And it is through the efforts of men like Jack Goggin that we learn our history. The diffident, quietly spoken local schoolteacher became for me, and I suspect for many other Merthyr children, what his fellow citizen, the historian, Gwyn Alf Williams was for Wales: the People's Remembrancer.

# EAST

## THE WHITEY

The Whitey, the White Tip, officially labelled the Dowlais Great Tip, loomed on the Penydarren skyline like a vast, misshapen moon. Up closer, this mountain of grey-white slag resembled a beached Moby Dick or a single-tier wedding cake that had been trodden on and kicked through the mud. Its huge crags, steep cliffs, overhangs, narrow cwms and traverses were as impressive as a Himalayan massif. The play of the evening sun on its bulging contours produced enchanting displays of soft pink, honey and purple light.

The Whitey was the product of sixty years of waste from the Bessemer steelmaking furnaces at Dowlais, dumped there daily until the works closed in 1930. The freshly layered molten slag lit up the sky, turning night into day and invoking the same awe in visitors as that provoked in that intrepid tourist, George Borrow, by his first sight of Cyfarthfa's fiercely-burning tips one night in 1854.

By the early Fifties when I and my friends played in its shadow, the Whitey's white hot slopes had cooled, but it continued to fire our imaginations. It was a sinister place on the cusp of enchantment and fear. A cave halfway up its bulging southern slope drew us as if to the mouth of Hell. Those who dared climb to its summit plateau found themselves in a black wilderness where ingots of slag, petrified as it poured from its containers, stood like prehistoric megaliths as mysterious as Stonehenge. The plateau was riven with crevasses, some big enough to swallow unsuspecting victims. Smoke, so we imagined, still wreathed through the cracks from its molten belly.

The Whitey dominated an industrial wasteland which may have been a blight, a reminder of past prosperity and present misery, for our parents. But for us it was a playground of limitless possibilities. The bed of a railway track, which had once fed the Dowlais Works with iron ore from Cardiff and carried Dowlais products to the world, still skirted the base of the tip. Its decaying embankments and ruined bridges became our Wild West forts, desert outposts of the French Foreign Legion, a battleground on which to re-enact Waterloo. A twist of rusted rail became a steed on which to fight King Arthur's battles; an abandoned coal truck a galleon on which to sail the Seven Seas, or a spaceship. The great rolling mills of the Dowlais Works, which had once spewed out rails to web continents, had given way to new factories. BSA, Birmingham Small Arms, ran a gun factory there during World War II. After the war, the land around it turned into a dump for redundant army vehicles – rusting jeeps, broken-down lorries, even tanks. We spent weeks, months, years, working out how to burrow beyond its chain fence to reach such promising food for our fantasies. We would spend all day in this paradise, our mothers anxiously scanning the horizon for our return long before we walked back down the mountain to reality.

Today's children have no such luck. The area has been sterilised of its dereliction, its history, its fascination. The great white whale of the Whitey has gone, broken up to form the foundations of anonymous motorways. Reclamation and opencast mining has gouged out decaying buildings, disused railway tracks, old bridges and embankments, the last romantic reminders of a fecund industrial past. They have changed forever the contours of the land, creating a landscape as flat and as unnaturally green as an artificial football pitch. A dual carriageway, the A4060, the slip road by-passing Merthyr on its way to Abergavenny, now slices through what was once the Whitey. A handful of neatly landscaped, clinically white modern factories occupy the sites of the rolling mills.

And yet this transformation from the unsightly but fruitful chaos of history to a modern sterility has brought unexpected rewards. Land on which the Whitey once stood has become a recreation ground where people come to walk and exercise their dogs. Its eastern edge rises to the embankment carrying the new road. Beyond, the ground rises past the derelict tips of coal mines that once fed the Dowlas Works to the majestic wilderness of Merthyr Common, rising to 1500ft above sea level. A plantation of young trees covers the road embankment. Between it and the recreation ground rises a series of recently-sown copses. And there, miraculously, on ground which so recently epito-

mised the achievements and decay of our industrial past, you can find the symbol of Wales's regeneration as a natural wilderness. Red kites, the delicate white lacework beneath the 10ft span of their wings visible against the sun, soar into the morning sky. Their call, kiaw, kiaw, is as unmistakable on the crystal summer air as the blast of the steam whistle that once called men, women and children to their shifts in the

ironworks which had invented that whistle.

The kites have been so persistent that it is obvious they have nested nearby. I have watched one, perched on a fence pole feet from the thunder of the slip road, totally indifferent to the whine of cars and the roar of lorries. And yet the huge amber eyes staring from the grey-white head were as alert as radar to potential prey, food for his young. The kites are not the only birds of prey to grace this no-man's land between rural and urban Wales. Clouds of buzzards, the fan of their dense tails clearly visible, tumble and cavort above the trees as if in some joyous dance of courtship. Hawks hover above the waste-land east of the road, ceaselessly searching for prey.

Not all welcome these newcomers. I watched squads of magpies rise to intercept the elegantly circling kites, driving them away, fearful of what the dangerous raptors might do to their young. Birds, it seems, are as resentful as Man of the intrusions of foreigners. Once the Welsh displayed the same frenzied resentment of the Irish they believed had come to take their jobs in Dowlais. The kites may be symbols of a greener Merthyr rising from the spoil tips of its indus-trial past, but the battles they re-enact are as old as history.

Now, as I write in February 2008, man's meddling is once again reshaping the landscape. The giant Ffos-y-Fran opencast mining scheme, lasting seventeen years, is swallowing up the land east of the Slip Road. With it will go much of what remains of Merthyr's indus-trial heritage. And with it will disappear the kites, the hawks and the buzzards, perhaps for a generation, perhaps for ever.

## THE OLD SLIP ROAD

The road climbing the waste-land of East Merthyr starts nowhere and ends in nothing, like the motorways that begin the march across the mountains of southern Italy and then vanish as if by a stroke of Harry Potter's wand. Those elegant monuments to Italian profligacy, bleaching in the sun like the bones of Mafia victims, are the products of organised crime whose greed is matched by its laziness. The godfathers use a little of massive government grants to begin public projects before walking away, their pockets jangling with the rest. But this Merthyr highway is a spectre from the past rather than a symbol of contemporary corruption.

I remember the building of the A4060 Slip Road in the early 1950s largely because it spelled the end of the untroubled sleep of childhood. The road by-passed Merthyr on its way from Cardiff to Abergavenny and the English Midlands. Before that everything, from the draymen's horse-drawn wagons to the roaring long-distance trucks, passed along the road that ran through the centre of Merthyr, up through Penydarren and on to Dowlais. I slept above my father's café in Penydarren which stood the width of a narrow pavement – perhaps a yard and a half – away from that road. The noise, like the low rumble of thunder, was incessant. But it soothed me to sleep like a lullaby. Then, just as I was preparing for the eleven plus that would decide the rest of my life, the Slip Road opened. Much of the traffic moved there and I found it impossible to sleep through the raucous silence.

The new road may not have had the beauty of arched and pillared Italian highways running swiftly through rugged mountains, but it picked its way through the left-overs of the Industrial Revolution with careful precision. To its right, as it swept up the valley east of the town, was the tangle of railway lines and bridges that had once fed the Dowlais Iron and Steelworks and which still carried passengers and the products of Dowlais's offspring, the Ivor Works. Beyond them, stretching to the horizon, were the rounded spoil tips of the innumerable coal pits and iron mines that had serviced Dowlais and its neighbour, the Penydarren Ironworks. To its left, forcing the road to curve sharply round it, loomed the massive presence of the Dowlais Great Tip, 'The Whitey'. More than forty years after the Slip Road opened the tip was carted away for road-fill. The road took advantage of the reclaimed land to grow into four lanes and a two-mile stretch was straightened to slice through what had once been the mountain of grey-white slag.

But few locals seem to know that the by-passed stretch of the old road had avoided the ignominies of the excavators. It has survived as if preserved in aspic. Almost fifteen years after the flow of cars abruptly stopped, the white lines along its centre are as fresh as if they had been painted last month. A cat's eye occasionally winks from its holder. The kerbs are sharp and intact, contemptuous of the odd thistle forcing through the concrete. Even the patchwork of tarmac repairs look freshly made.

The old road springs as if from underground into the embankment fifteen feet above and only a few yards to the east of its replacement. It runs gently up hill for two miles, gradually veering by as much as half a mile from the new road. Then, as it begins to merge with its replacement once more, it ends in a tangle of grass and broken concrete. But if journeys along this forlorn highway now lead nowhere, it can at least provide a pathway to the past.

A two-in-one bridge carries the road below what was once Dowlais Junction, one of the most important sections of Merthyr's complex railways. Here a branch line from the Dowlais Works met the passenger and goods line from Dowlais and the Ivor Works. The joint line travelled on to the mountain-top village of Cwmbargoed, then plunged into the beautiful valley of the Taff Bargoed before continuing to Nelson and Cardiff. Its climb to the 1500 ft summit of the wild Merthyr Common made it one of the steepest and most dangerous in Wales. It was built to carry imported iron ore from the port of Cardiff to Dowlais in an increasingly desperate bid to keep the huge works open once the local ore had been exhausted. Millions of tons travelled along this line, each journey requiring several engines to pull the line of heavy trucks . The bridge still carries the graffiti that once urged travellers to find salvation – 'Jesus Saves', 'God is Love'. These days, their only audience are flocks of ragged sheep.

Now as I write early in 2008, many months after I first discovered this brief journey into history, it may have finally been consigned there. The important complex of rail and industrial remains it bordered is rapidly disappearing into the maw of the Ffos-y-Fran opencast scheme. That remnant of road may have already suffered the same fate. True to form, Merthyr is once again devouring its past with gluttonous alacrity.

## FFOS-Y-FRAN

Hang-gliders dance a stately quadrille above a ridge lemon-yellow in the late autumn sun. Beneath a cobalt sky darkening into night, a narrow road arrows across the high plateau towards mountains that climb the horizon, steps to the roof of the world. Horses graze relentlessly on the coarse grass, tufted with reeds, ignoring the cars that whine over a cattle grid just yards away. The horses are the true inheritors of this bleak beauty at the summit of the South Wales Valleys. For almost two millennia they gathered here in their hundreds several times a year for the sales which were the heart of the great fairs held here. For men, too, this remote spot just a few miles from the centres of Merthyr and Dowlais became a refuge and a temple in which they celebrated their humanity. These bare acres were their civic forum where they gathered to assert their sense of community, their lust for freedom, their determination to defend their human dignity with their lives if necessary. And it was. They came here to Twyn-y-Waun in their thousands during the uprising of 1831. They came to listen to their leaders, safe from ironmasters and their soldiers, to gather their strength and reaffirm their dangerous commitment to the struggle for a better society.

It is a landscape that has become as familiar to me as it was for a nineteenth century rebel; a landscape that, having survived the past encroachments of civilisation, the depredations of iron and coal mining and opencast 'reclamation', seemed touched with a timeless serenity. Until now. Until the appearance of the latest threat which could do more damage than the iron and coal mines and the arrival

of the railway and the motor car. It will change the bleak, bare beauty of Twyn-y-Waun and its highland for a generation, perhaps for ever. Already, a bile-black vomit of rock and soil, just a few hundred yards from Twyn-y-Waun, has added a new silhouette to the horizon. Alongside it, the arm of the vivid yellow excavator that helped to create it slithers and falls and rises, as rhythmically as an act of masturbation.

The freshly dug mound, as yet only a fraction of its eventual size, is the outer edge of the vast Ffos-y-Fran opencast mining scheme that will tear almost 11m tonnes of coal out of 1,000 acres of the valley roof. Twyn-y-Waun, so central to the past life of Merthyr Tydfil, will border a series of holes reaching a depth of up to 600ft, into which will disappear much of what remains of Merthyr's proud industrial history and wildlife. Here, day after day little more than twelve months ago, I watched a pair of majestic red kites slowly wheel and hover and glide through the mountain air. I saw them swoop to perch on the fence posts that border the A4060 slip road forming the western edge of the vast Ffos-y-Fran scheme. I watched them watching me with a cold, imperious, yellow gaze. I climbed through the eerie, resonant landscape of grassed-over coal tips and dirt roads and the overgrown beds of pioneering railways and saw falcons circle slowly, scrutinising every inch of the land below for prey. Now huge, vividly yellow dumper trucks nosed with black snout through the earth like giant slugs.

The industrial remains on the site hark back to the earliest days of the iron and coal mining needed to feed the voracious appetite of the rapidly expanding Dowlais and Penydarren Ironworks. The Glamorgan-Gwent Archaeological Trust said on its website before the arrival of the massive trucks and diggers that Ffos-y-Fran was "an extensive and nationally important landscape of industrial sites associated with the Dowlais Ironworks, mainly comprising features associated with iron ore extraction and, to a lesser extent, coal, and in use between the late eighteenth century and early nineteenth century. The area is characterised by extractive features (mainly waste tips), the Dowlais Free Drainage System associated with the Dowlais and later the Ivor Ironworks, and mineral railways and tramways as well as public rail (now disused)".

The new scheme is designated 'reclamation' of derelict land. Miller Argent, the mining company, claims much of it is dangerous, although only one man has died through ground collapse there in more than fifty years, a record which accident prevention experts would yearn for as they survey the carnage on our roads. The 'reclamation', its critics maintain, is opencast mining in all but name. Clearing up the derelict land and making it safe would take a fraction of the time the current enterprise will last. And less than eighty per cent of the land involved in the scheme can be classified as derelict. Ffos-y-Fran is the third part of a 'reclamation' programme which had previously torn 1.22m tonnes of coal out of this once breathtakingly beautiful part of East Merthyr. The scale of this latest enterprise takes my breath away. The site dominating the Merthyr valley from its heights on the roof of the valley will be mined for at least seventeen years. A further five may be needed to ensure the area is recontoured. My family home is within a kilometre down the valley. But there is a very good chance I will be dead by the time Ffos-y-Fran is fully 'restored', perhaps into the sterile, plastic landscape that characterises so many 'restored' opencast areas in Wales. The critics who determinedly oppose exploitation of the site point to the possible effects of the huge scheme on the health of those who live close-by; the centre of Merthyr is less than two kilometres away. Planning permission was obtained despite the fact that people live within forty metres of the opencast boundary fence.

Miller Argent has proved sensitive to the complaints that so much of Merthyr's history is likely to disappear in their excavators' buckets. They say they will save several scheduled ancient monuments, a listed structure – a timber aqueduct – and at least part of the Dowlais Free Drainage System, an ingenious piece of early nineteenth century civil engineering, consisting of storage ponds and waterways that enabled the Dowlais Ironworks to gather the water it needed to drive its machinery.

The company has said it has even sited its northern overburden mound, storing soil and rock removed to mine the coal and eventually destined to refill a massive hole, away from the 'presumed site' of the Waun Fair. The black mound of rock and soil I saw in full view of the site makes that gesture meaningless. Miller Argent recognises that it will not be able to save much of what is of archaeological and heritage value at Ffos-y-Fran. And by removing the context in which they worked, the value of those artefacts saved will be much reduced. As part of its concessions to bodies such as the Countryside Council for Wales, Miller Argent has agreed to back a comprehensive archaeological survey involving the excavation and recording of sites and remains which will disappear into its black holes. The work has been contracted to the same Glamorgan-Gwent Trust. A press release on the trust's website in March 2008, said that those recorded included a "well-preserved steam-driven ironstone mine belonging to the early nineteenth century called the Soap Vein Pit, several mid-nineteenth century ironstone and coal mines, tramroads, railways...".

In stark contrast to this loss, it seems to me that the returns for the community from the operation will be extremely modest. Rates on coal extraction, plant and buildings will amount to £1m per year according to the planning inspector's report which gave the assent for the Ffos-y-Fran scheme in November 2004. A community fund will receive between £6.4m and £10.8m in royalties on the coal mined, according to the price of coal at the time of sale. Even at the top end that will amount to just £1 for every tonne of coal extracted. Merthyr will benefit from perhaps 200 jobs on the site, only some of which will be filled by local people, and up to 400 in spin-off industries.

More long-term benefits for the community could have been gained by preserving and developing the area for industrial tourism. Ffos-y-Fran, with its historic remains and its nearness to the sites of the Dowlais and Penydarren Ironworks, would have been the ideal spot for an industrial heritage park with visitor centres explaining what went on in those pioneering enterprises. Models incorporating industrial remains could have described precisely how the iron ore and coal needed by those ironworks were obtained. The 'well-preserved' Soap Vein Pit, about to disappear forever, might have been ideal for that. The remains of old tramways and railways would have proved irresistible to legions of railway enthusiasts. The successful celebrations of the 2004 bicentenary of Richard Trevithick's famous journey showed the powerful tourist appeal of railway history. The park could have provided more direct jobs than opencast and for a much longer period. Spin-offs in terms of hotel accommodation, restaurant visits and shopping would have made the estimated 400 indirect jobs provided by Miller Argent look like what it is, small economic beer. It is already too late.

Plans to create heritage attractions in other parts of history-rich Merthyr are rapidly disappearing. Six well-preserved late eighteenth century and early nineteenth century blast furnaces, on the site of what was once the Cyfarthfa Ironworks, were earmarked for an inter-national tourist attraction which could have incorporated Cyfarthfa Castle, its park, the nearby Pandy Farm and ironworkers' cottages and Joseph Parry's birthplace. The scheme could have attracted thousands more visitors each year. It was dealt a severe blow by the local authority's decision to locate a modern business and innovation centre on land that fronts the furnaces. Now even that idea has been abandoned after ground there was found to be contaminated. Fears persist that other areas rich in early social and industrial history will eventually succumb to plans for redevelopment or further bouts of open-cast 'reclamation'. All that remains for those who believe in the enormous economic and cultural potential of Merthyr's unique history is the odd isolated heritage trail, like that which traces the path of Trevithick's first railway journey.

Among the most wounding aspects of Ffos-y-Fran for me is the role played by the Welsh Assembly which, with the Merthyr Borough Council, has supported the scheme. Letters from Labour ministers in Westminster to the party's First Minister in Cardiff, Rhodri Morgan, revealed London's eagerness to exploit the coal reserves at Ffos-y-Fran in order, among other things, to keep the coal-fired Aberthaw Power Station near Barry open. That argument did nothing to endear the new mine or the Labour government to outraged environmentalists and climate change activists. Local groups have been loud in their opposition on a variety of grounds, including noise and air pollution and health issues. Despite that, the Welsh Assembly wasted no time in displaying its commitment to the project. Having endorsed its planning inspector's decision to approve the new mine, it immediately launched a successful appeal when the High Court overturned that decision. Nor should responsibility for nurturing a project which will destroy much of Merthyr's remaining industrial heritage rest solely with the Assembly's Labour administration. Plaid Cymru, The Party of Wales, was in government with Labour when another plea to withdraw planning permission for mining at Ffos-y-Fran was rejected.

# CENTRAL

## PENYDARREN – THE STINKY

A thin line of council houses tops the bank to the right of the new road as it sweeps past the roundabout, offering a few bushes and flowers as tokens of its greenness. To the left of the road the hill has the plastic neatness of land reclaimed from its industrial past. Its rustic gates, babbling brook, bite-sized wooden bridges, fish pond and paths climbing through clustered bushes betray the sterile imagination of the golf course architect. This is a landscape emptied of memory.

Refilling its blank panorama with its history is doubly difficult in a terrain which has been flattened as if by a bomb – shifted, recontoured, its jags and edges rubbed smooth. Only an isolated landmark remains, like Hiroshima's skeletal tower, to help you reconstruct the past. At the top of what was once Penydarren High Street, The Norton, the last of its eight public houses, still attracts a desultory clientele in day-glo tee-shirts, lycra shellsuits and cheap earrings glinting above tattooed arms and necks. Half a mile below, the steps still climb past the ugly modern shed of Horeb Chapel, shorn of the size and gloomy grace of its early Victorian predecessor, gutted by fire twenty years ago. Next to the roundabout, the foundations of an abandoned garage stand where once there was Hughes the Blacksmith's forge. Even with these points of reference my past remains evasive. My father's café should have been where now stands that blue and white bus stop. But the flattened tips, filled-in canyons and culverted river beds cloud my certainty. A few acres of ersatz rusticity have stolen a third of my life.

Absence defines this scene, created by the bulldozers and wrecking balls which reduced my childhood to rubble: absence of narrow streets, noisome slums, stinking rivers, pubs, chattering neighbours, yowling children, quarrelling drunks, lowering slag tips, ruined railways, dog shit, dead sheep, mud and clutter; absence of community.

On its left, where the brook now burbles below its bijou bridges, Penydarren High Street was flanked by a landscape produced by Merthyr's world-shaping industrial revolution. At the bottom of the valley, perhaps one hundred feet below the High Street, ran the old Tramroad, the first of those which once webbed the village. It carried products from the Dowlais Ironworks, two miles above Penydarren, to the Glamorgan Canal two and half miles below in Merthyr, then on to Cardiff and the world. Later, it brought iron from Dowlais and Penydarren onto to the new Merthyr Tramroad, Trevithick's tramroad, which by-passed the canal at Merthyr, connecting with it instead at Abercynon eight miles down the valley. By 1832, a harbinger of a new age, the powerful, Neath-built engine named Perseverance rattled and snorted and gasped down this line to Abercynon, terrifying onlookers with the soot and flames belching from its narrow chimney. Those brave enough or desperate enough could pay a penny to travel on trucks piled high with iron. It was Wales's first sustained taste of the railway era.

Beyond the Tramroad flowed the Morlais Brook which for the first two miles of its course from the foothills of the Brecon Beacons ran with the sweet-tasting clarity of a mountain stream. By the time it reached Penydarren, four miles from its source, it had become so polluted by its upstream chemical works and factories – and by us – that the stench of rotten eggs and the rotting carcasses of cats and dogs rose from it like swamp gas. For us it had long since become The Stinky and the threat that terrorised us, as we hopped gingerly across its stepping stones, was that if we fell into its yellow scum shot with greens and reds and blues it would strip the flesh from us like a shoal of barracuda. If we survived the water and its poisons, the rats that, so we imagined, swarmed through its debris awaited us.

The tips created by the Dowlais and Penydarren Ironworks rose steeply from left bank of the Morlais. Their grassed-over slopes towered three hundred feet above the river, our Alps or Himalayas to be climbed and then slid down, clinging to the cardboard beneath our backsides, praying we would not tumble into the river and the waiting rats. Those tips, made of shiny, brittle rock ebonised by the furnaces, were my companions throughout childhood and adolescence. They offered a viewing platform onto my world. From their flat summits, I could see north beyond Dowlais to the jagged Beacons stencilling the horizon. To the south lay the soft green hills of the Taff Valley and Cardiff. The tips nourished our imaginations. They were the stage on which we could transform into explorers trekking through arctic wastes, Arthur and his medieval knights, big game hunters prowling through the African savannah. They were sources of pain as I slogged up their slopes training for school rugby. And on the long summer days of adolescence they were a refuge where I could nurture my appetite for literature on the sweaty gothic romance of Dennis Wheatley's novels with titles like *To The Devil A Daughter*, or *The Devil Rides Out.*

In a hollow south of the tips once stood the reason why Penydarren had not remained a wild and scattered sheep farm. Here in 1784 a Staffordshire ironmaster, Francis Homfray, and his three sons established the fourth and last of the giant works that would make Merthyr the greatest iron manufacturing centre of the world. It was the smallest and poorest in mineral resources. But for a while it out-produced rivals like neighbouring Dowlais. The works' handicaps ensured its closure in 1859. By then it had spawned the High Street and satellites like Company Row, a colourful, quarrelsome ghetto of Irish workers that had stood behind my home in Mathias Terrace. By the time I was born Company Row or 'Cump' as we knew it – I used to think it was an exotic Welsh nickname – was already a decaying ruin.

It bequeathed us a wasteland which became a wonderland, a place where we played hide-and-seek, marbles, football, cricket or built our guys and bonfires. There, I was kicked by the coal merchant's horse after I had dared to run too close to its hind legs as, tethered to a wall, it grazed its hay. Despite such hazards and its broken walls, piles of rubble and a steep drop into the tramroad below, 'Cump' gave us a chance to grow up safely and confidently. It was the place where we began the more lasting of life's lessons. Here we played doctors and nurses with the girls as, pants and knickers down, we explored with the alacrity of innocence the differences between each others' bodies.

## PENYDARREN HIGH STREET

To walk down Penydarren High Street in the Fifties and Sixties was to peer into purgatory. The street was Penydarren's beating heart, a row of narrow terraced cottages punctuated by glowering chapels, cavernous public houses and, above all, shops and workshops. Through them flowed all you needed for a decent life. You could even shoe your horse at the blacksmiths. In a single section, built just before World War I and grandly named Mathias Terrace, a dozen businesses formed a shopping precinct long before the concept was invented. There you could find a hairdresser, two butchers, a grocer, a greengrocer, newsagent, Chemist, an Italian fish shop, Barsi's, an

Italian café, Basini's and, for a while, a cinema, the Cosy, with its grand, mock marble façade and flea-infested seats where my teenager sisters absently-mindedly nursed me and my younger brother in shawls while, enthralled, they watched Errol Flynn, Gary Cooper and Clark Gable make love to Olivia de Haviland, Claudette Colbert and Claire Trevor.

The community which grew along the High Street and its feeder streets inhabited a self-contained world in which a medley of races and religions, from Eastern European Jewish to Italian Catholic, harmonised into a colourful whole. Headmistresses, miners, draymen, council labourers, insurance salesmen, civil servants, the unemployed and of course, small businessmen and women, drank, ate, loved, laughed and cried together. They attended each other's weddings and funerals and went on holiday together, to Barry Island on the train or, on another train, to Pontsarn, three miles and world away from their grimy streets. There, in a wooded hollow in what is now the Beacon Beacons National Park, beneath the soaring symmetry of the railway viaduct, the women and their children picnicked and paddled in the Taff Fechan River, gurgling over its limestone bed while the men trudged up the hill to the Abermorlais pub and a day on the beer. The more adventurous boys would slip into their swimming trunks and sidle off to the little bridge two hundred yards away below which the river plunged twenty feet into a narrow ravine guarded by sharp slabs of rock. They would crouch, poised like the cliff divers of Acapulco, on the parapet before plunging into the icy river, pulling in their stomachs to avoid the rocks.

Penydarren High Street's reference points were the eight pubs that measured out its mile and a half. From the ponderous, red-bricked Norton Tavern to the cavernous Crystal Palace the street plunged steeply before briefly flattening out between the Crystal and the Talbot, once a stop-over for the Abergavenny and London stage coach. Then it tumbled once more to the Musical Hall and into Merthyr itself.

Each pub had its own architectural style and drinking culture. Some were basic drinking dens, their bars the converted front rooms of terraced houses where cider was served straight from its barrel. By contrast, the Talbot was an elegant coaching inn with a history predating the area's swift industrialisation. Others, like the Crystal Palace, named for the site of the Great Exhibition, were High Victorian temples to the art – often as obsessively followed as a religion – of alcohol consumption; with tall, ornately-ceilinged bars, sensuously curved wooden counters behind which rose tall shelves packed with glittering glasses, ceramic whisky barrels and row after row of bottles. Each establishment bound its customers with the iron loyalties of family. Nothing short of a catastrophic souring of the beer or a hefty hike in prices or a quarrel with the landlord would drive a drinker out of his favourite pub. When someone did change their allegiance, scandalised gossip rippled through this obsessive, self-referential world.

The presence of so many places forbidden to us children meant that they exercised a powerful pull on our imaginations. Like most of his friends, my father followed a drinking routine as formal as a ritual. For forty years he drank six days a week – Sundays it was closed – in the sawdust-floored bar of the Crystal Palace, which flanked the northern end of Mathias Terrace. Its twin, terminating the terrace's march south, was the Talbot. Each lunchtime and evening my father downed a pint, perhaps two, of bitter, a bottle, perhaps two, of Worthington White Label, and, occasionally, a whisky chaser. The landlord and his friend, Charlie Thomas, knew just when to offer him the pint, the bottle or the shot of whisky. Perhaps once every five or six years, they quarrelled and my father huffed the two hundred yards down to the Talbot for a month or two. When he was in residence and needed back at the shop I would be dispatched to fetch him.

To swing through the heavy, etched glass doors of the Crystal's bar was to embark on a fleeting rite of passage. Like a first taste of beer, that glimpse of the male adult world awaiting me repelled more than it attracted. Fifty years on, I remember vividly the shock of blunt, familiar faces in unfamiliar surroundings: the heavy tables, the tall windows, the polished bar dominated by its rows of brass beer pumps and their voluptuous ceramic handles. I felt an intruder disturbing a sect in the middle of a secret liturgy. Above all, I remember the smell, the sourness of the unwashed male, pungent on the sickly sweet stench of hoppy beer and days-old tobacco smoke. If it made me want to vomit, I knew that, sooner or later, I would make the closed, self-absorbed rite of the drinker my own.

The High Street was the oldest part of Penydarren, having grown with the ironworks which gave birth to the village in the mid eighteenth century. It contained one of Merthyr's oldest Irish ghettoes, families who, after generations as society's pariahs, had been dumped into more or less permanent unemployment and, often, habitual drunkenness. Their small, damp hovels pitched down the steep slope of the top of the street. A fungus of cramped alleyways and cellars spread behind them. My route to and from my Catholic primary school in Dowlais took me past their front doors often gapingly open to encourage a little ventilation. I was already aware of the gulf between my secure universe and theirs. I would glance in guiltily, eager for a glimpse of that other world.

And there on hot summer's days, through an open door, I would be punished for my curiosity with the vision of a boy, perhaps two or three years older than me, so badly crippled he could not rise unaided from the bed placed in full view of that door. I remember the gaunt white mask of suffering that was his face, the huge eyes blazing from sunken cheeks, his stiff, claw-like limbs. I want to remember my sympathetic smile to him. I suspect I only managed a furtive glance of shock and guilt. Sometimes I would see his heroic family labouring to manoeuvre his twisted, useless body in its huge, bed-like wheelchair down steep and decaying steps in a bid to give him a little freedom and to feed his starved imagination. The question still haunts me. What could he have done to deserve that bleak life-sentence of poverty and crippling disease? The Merthyr that offered so many of us a chance to grow, to go out and challenge the world, was for others a tomb from which the only release was death.


## 6 MATHIAS TERRACE

I was eight or nine when my best friend, a keen Boy Scout, asked my mother, Marina, why she wouldn't allow me to join the movement. She replied she had had enough of uniforms to last her a lifetime. Her hatred of the paraphernalia of military life had nothing to do with her family's way of making a living. There had been, as far as I know, no professional soldiers among her ancestors. Nor did she lack physical courage. When, on Saturday nights, the pubs which flanked our street like bookends spewed their customers out on to the street, they flocked to our café for Oxos – beef teas – and hot steamed steak and kidney pies. Often, their drink-fuelled boisterousness would suddenly darken and the whole place would erupt in violence. A big powerful woman, Marina would roll up her sleeves, plant my brother and me, still toddlers, on the big ice cream fridge out of harm's way and join my father wading through the upturned chairs and tables to the fighting, gouging customers. Within minutes the shop would be emptied, locked and shuttered.

But by the time she had married and moved to the little café at 6

Mathias Terrace, Penydarren, she had learned that a boyish, patriotic enthusiasm for flags and colourful uniforms sometimes exacted a terrible price.

She was one of seven surviving children of a comparatively prosperous small mountain farmer, in the Northern Italian Apennines, whose fortunes had been boosted when her three brothers arrived as boys to work in the Italian cafés of South Wales. By the time she joined them in 1924, a wild-eyed young peasant woman with a mass of unruly hair, they were already carving out a small business empire for themselves. As they moved into the 1930s the Basinis of the Rhondda – my mother and my father shared a surname even before they married – owned a chain of half a dozen shops including two fish and chip shops, two cafés and a couple of grocery stores.

By the time World War II approached, Marina had become an indispensable part of the business. She and her brothers had been joined by the youngest member of the family, a breathtakingly handsome young man with huge brown eyes called Bartolomeo, or Bert as he was known in the Rhondda. Three of the brothers were married with children, some of whom were already teenagers. Like almost all the young men in South Wales's substantial Italian community, they had been impressed by the loud, extravagant promises of the bombastic Benito Mussolini.

As small businessmen struggling to make a living, almost none of them were interested in politics. Only one or two understood what Fascism stood for and supported Mussolini with Blackshirt conviction. But, as patriotic Italians, they loved the way the dictator had made the name of Italy reverberate around the world as a power to be reckoned with. They had in the past felt isolated and ignored as an exiled community, treated with indifference by successive Italian governments. Mussolini's regime, in stark contrast, had wooed them, establishing clubs and Italian schools throughout Britain in an effort to teach their offspring Italian culture and the language and to make them feel a cherished part of the wider fascist Italy.

Many, including my father and my uncles, sent their children to these weekend schools where they sang songs, learned a little Italian and dressed in the uniforms of the fascist youth organisations like the Balilla. The Italian regime established clubs, Fasci, in the urban centres of England, Scotland and Wales. One opened in Cardiff in 1936. They were social clubs as well as centres of fascist propaganda, where members could meet, have a glass of wine, play cards and reminisce.

When Mussolini in a ranting, combative speech declared war on Britain on June 10, 1940 what had been a largely innocent, apolitical expression of patriotism became a matter of life and death for the Italians of South Wales. In the next few days riots attacking Italian businesses broke out in towns and cities throughout Britain. In Wales they erupted in Swansea and in the Rhondda. Among their targets were shops owned by my mother and her family. By then the British government had struck. Thousands of Italians, including my father and two of my mother's brothers, were arrested and interned, locked up in a filthy, rat-infested, disused flour mill in the north of England. My father, who had fought with Britain and her allies in the First World War and had been badly wounded, and one of my uncles were eventually taken to camps on the Isle of Man. They were released a few months later.

A more terrible fate awaited the darling of my mother's eye, the baby of the family, the doe-eyed Bartolomeo. Recently-married, he was the father of twins less than a year old when the police knocked on his door. Instead of being sent with his brother to the Isle of Man he was earmarked for a camp in Canada and, along with 1563 other men, he found himself on a converted luxury liner, the *Arandora Star*, sailing out of Liverpool. Around 734 of them were Italian. The rest were German – Jewish refugees from Hitler's Germany as well as Nazis – and British servicemen. At 7am on July 1, 1940 the ship was torpedoed by a German U-boat, 125 miles off the coast of Ireland. Less than 300 of the Italians survived. My uncle Bert was not among them. It was months before his family knew of his fate.

My mother never recovered from the blow. Up to her death, more than forty years later, she would brim with tears every time his name was mentioned. I cannot imagine the pain my mother and her family suffered during this time of uncertainty, isolation and terrible loss. It seems to me, the price my relatives had to pay was out of all propor-tion to their 'crime' of expressing a patriotic affection for their country and for a regime that seemed to care about them. The notion underpinning the Churchill government's policy of internment, that this group of fish-shop owners and café proprietors represented a genuine threat to the security of the state, is palpably absurd.

But Marina never allowed the tragedy to dominate the rest of her life. Instead, soon after she accepted the biggest challenge of her life. When he had been interned my father, a widower, had been forced to leave three children ranging from eleven to fifteen with no idea of what would happen to them. After he had been released he courted my mother, whom he had wooed many years before. As a successful businesswoman in her early forties, the most sensible decision she could have made was, perhaps, to say no. Instead, with what seems to me now enormous courage, she said yes, moved to a town she had never seen before and took on the responsibility of raising three traumatised, hurt and rebellious children. Within three years she had two of her own.

## 6 MATHIAS TERRACE – THE WOUNDS OF WAR

They looked, beneath the thin, translucent skin of my father's legs, like plump raisins in a pudding dough. They moved, seemingly retaining a little of the velocity with which they sprang from the German mortar shell more than fifty years before. When they reached the surface, encrusted with debris like salvage from the sea, you could pick them like grapes. For most of his adult life Marco, my father, lived with the shrapnel that had peppered his legs as he fought the Germans and the Austrians in the high Italian mountains during the First World War. The surgeons who had treated him for three months in the hospital in Padua, near Venice, had removed as many pieces as they could, leaving the rest to nature. He had been one of the Alpini, the crack mountain troops that even the most xenophobic German or English military minds admitted were among the best soldiers in that war.

When Italy entered the war on the British and French side in April, 1915, he had been a young man working in cafés in Aberdare and Mountain Ash. When he was called up for the Italian Army, he was marched off to a coal ship leaving Cardiff for Genoa and handed over to the military authorities when he reached the Italian port, thirty miles as the crow flies from the village where he was born. He had many stories to tell of his three years on the Allied side, in a war often fought in the arctic wilderness of peaks rising to 14,000 ft, where frostbite and hunger were bigger threats than enemy bullets. Some were horrific, some funny. The most effective combined both.

When, for example, his battalion was involved in the Italian retreat that followed defeat by the Germans and Austrians at Caporetto in the shadow of the Julian Alps in 1917, he and a handful of his companions found themselves fleeing through the fertile plains of Friuli Venezia Giulia, north of Venice. The locals fled before them. In one rapidly-abandoned town, where the shops were still stuffed with goods and the banks with cash, they were captured by the pursuing Germans. They managed to turn the tables on their captors by taking them into a fully-stocked osteria, a local pub, and getting them drunk. As they began to usher their prizes south towards the reforming Italian lines they could not resist the temptation to visit a bank and 'rescue' some of the cash. When they eventually reached their lines, they were decorated for capturing a numerically superior enemy force and imprisoned for looting! It was, whatever its truth, a good story.

The price that shell exacted from him, apart from those three months in hospital, was a lifetime of pain. I would watch, with the same combination of fascination and horror I listened to his war stories, as he prepared to clean his wounds. He would take a bowl and sit in his armchair to unwind the bandages he always wore. Often he would bathe his wounds in olive oil since that seemed to ease his discomfort. He never complained, nor did he allow those wounds to handicap him. He would walk for miles with the aid of his stick, taking me and my brother on expeditions into the foothills of the Beacons. I remember years later, when I was in my early twenties and he was into his seventies, accompanying him on a long trip home in Italy. When we went for walks lasting hours, into the mountain that rose to 5,000ft behind his village, I struggled to keep up with that swiftly-moving walking stick.

When it came to the Second World War, his service in the cause of the Allies counted for little. A widower with young children, his only connection with fascist Italy was to send his children once or twice to the Italian school at nearby Pontypridd where they learned a little Italian. At 6am on June 11, 1940, the day after Mussolini declared war, a police inspector and a constable hammered on the door of the café in Mathias Terrace he had moved into less than four years before. They took him off to internment with little more than the clothes he stood in, while his children, terrified and uncomprehending, wept on the stairs. After stays at Maindy Barracks in Cardiff and in the stinking, rat-infested, disused Warth Cotton Mill near Bury, Lancashire, he was taken to an internment camp in the Isle of Man. Meanwhile his children were farmed out to Italian families, some of whom were more interested in a source of cheap labour than the children's welfare.

He later said little about his comparatively short spell at the sea-front camp in Douglas, the capital of the Isle of Man, except that it made him an expert draughts player, a skill he delighted in demonstrating. He never mentioned the hurt and the agonised anxiety over the fate of his children he must have felt. He was well-loved in Penydarren before and after his imprisonment. He brought my mother, in her forties and never before married, home as his new bride shortly after his release. When, less than a year later, she began to give birth to me, the neighbours hurried to help her through her labour. The friendships formed then would last my parents their lifetimes. But my father never lost his resentment at his treatment by the Britain that had been his first home since he had arrived here as an eight year-old.

Nor did he lose the raw physical courage he had displayed during that First World War. On the many occasions when local hard men tried to create havoc in the café, he never hesitated to tackle them, invariably besting them with a display of his ferocious determination. But it was courage of a different sort that impressed me most.

Always the loving, encouraging father, generous to a fault with his children and his friends, he twice lived through the death of a wife and faced up to the difficult task of looking after his children single-handedly. When he watched my mother die slowly and painfully, he was already approaching his seventies, an age at which many men would have given up under the force of yet another hammer blow and sink into torpor. But the youngest of his six children, myself and my brother, were nineteen and seventeen and still needed him. He responded magnificently, taking over responsibilities such as cooking for the family – he was, like my mother, an excellent cook – with great heart. I loved him for that above all else.

## BASINI'S CAFÉ – TEACHER BESSIE

If it was the comfort of the familiar you were looking for, as you groped your way into each morning, then Teacher Bessie was not the most reassuring sight to greet you. Above his blue boiler suit and black tee-shirt the transvestite dustman's plump, round face wore full make-up. The large eyes beneath the false eyelashes floated on seas of blue or black mascara. His lips beneath the rouged cheeks were soft cushions of vermilion to match his painted fingernails which never seemed to chip, as he emptied dustbin after heavy dustbin into the back of his lorry.

We lived above and beneath my parents' café, and as I tottered from my upstairs bedroom through the shop towards the living room on the floor below, he was already sitting down with his mates to a breakfast of tea and toast or perhaps a steamed steak and kidney pie. He was a large, heavy man with dyed black hair and surprisingly small and delicate feet and hands. His voice had the querulous vibrato of Dame Edith Evans playing Lady Bracknell in *The Importance of Being Ernest*. His gestures, the way he fluttered his eyelashes, puckered his mouth or sculpted his hands, had the exaggerated femininity of the drag artist he was away from his dustman's day job. He performed in various Merthyr workingmen's clubs, reserving the stage name, Teacher Bessie – which suggested the dominatrix who demanded complete obedience from her 'pupils' – for his more prosaic venues. In the posher clubs and private parties he became 'Madame Sonia'. But if, while he performed, he tolerated the raucous humour of his audiences and even the odd bawdy caress from an admirer, offstage no-one dared to take such liberties.

He had a deserved reputation as a strong man with a quick temper, more than capable of looking after himself even in Merthyr's emphatically masculine culture. Born, prosaically, Willie Pugh, he had worked as a blacksmith and in what remained of the Dowlais Ironworks before becoming a dustman to keep body and soul together. As I staggered through the café, bleary-eyed with sleep, I did my best to avoid staring at him, as much out of fear as politeness. But he was impossible to ignore and when my gaze was inevitably drawn towards him he would turn his slow, lazy eyes away, contemptuous of my curiosity. It is a measure of the humanity of 'Macho Merthyr' that his presence in the town was accepted with amused tolerance and understanding. He never, as far as I know, provoked persecution or even mild condemnation.

If Teacher Bessie was the most exotic of the characters that paraded through my father's small café between 7.30 in the morning and 11 at night, there were plenty of others to keep the curious fully engaged. Much of Merthyr's motley humanity passed through there from politicians and professional footballers to world boxing champions, priests, doctors, teachers, milkmen, coalmen, drunks, future mayors, pinball experts, slot machine addicts.

Merthyr's flotsam – the alcoholics, the homeless, the psychically wounded – lapped through the café like a tide, to beg a cup of tea or a sandwich from my sympathetic mother and my two elder sisters. Some, like the flamboyant, wildly handsome Bernard, became personal friends. Mostly drunk, his mind reputedly scarred at the hands of the Japanese in World War II, Bernard scattered ideas around like a machine gun. A handful hit the target long enough to sustain an intense and cheerfully rowdy argument. He had a rueful sense of the ridiculous which helped him to view the tragic gap between his potential and his wrecked reality without self-pity.

Among my father's friends was the tall, skeletal, homburg-hatted figure of S.O. Davies, Socialist and Welsh patriot, who had been Merthyr's MP for almost forty years. A dignified man of conscience who frequently refused to toe the official Labour line, he was loved and trusted even by those of his constituents, like my father, who did not share his politics. When, in the 1970 general election, the Labour Party dumped him on the grounds that at eighty-four he was too old, he stood as an Independent Labour candidate and thrashed his official party opponent, a colourless trade union functionary called Tal Lloyd.

A political chasm separated S.O. and my father. Like many small businessmen in the town, then and now, Marco was a Conservative whose political hero was Churchill, a fact that astonishes me since it was Churchill's insistence on locking up enemy aliens that had landed him in interment camps during the Second World War. My father's quixotically generous attitude to his persecutor was dangerous in a town whose attitude to the war leader was one of visceral hatred. Every time Churchill appeared on a cinema newsreel he was greeted with boos and howls of derision. He was still, among other sins, reviled as the man who sent in the troops to crush the Tonypandy strike of 1911.

I never shared my father's enthusiasm for the man who had locked him up, but I was enough my father's son to help found the Young Conservatives in Merthyr and to canvas for the party. It was, I tell myself now, the only way for a teenager to rebel in a town slavishly devoted to a Labour Party whose cynical representative too often treated it as a fiefdom to be exploited.

## BASINI'S CAFÉ – SALAMI AND STEAMED PIES

My father had his limitations as a cook. During the decades I worked with him in the family café I cannot remember him producing a piece of toast he had not burned or a plate of bacon and eggs that did not swim in fat. He was invariably the first of the family to get up, start two blazing coal fires – one in the café and one in the downstairs living room – and cook me a breakfast to see me off to school. Most of it, to my shame, would end up on the kitchen coal fire after he had disappeared upstairs.

But when it came to Italian cooking, his training in the Italian Army during the First World War stood him in good stead. He could create the most intricate and mouth-watering dishes. My mother was the mistress of pasta, smothering it with delicious sauces or stuffing it with melt-in-the mouth fillings. She would feed half the children of the street, including my friend Mansel Aylward, now Professor Aylward and at the end of a glittering career weighed down with honours. As an academic, senior government adviser and a key figure in the Welsh Health Service, he has travelled and eaten pasta all over the world. "The best I ever tasted," he still insists, "was your mother's". My father, on the other hand, was the master of the intricate salads. He would, with infinite patience, spend half an hour chopping the heart of a white cabbage into tender, mouth-watering slivers, adding spring onions, garlic, olive oil and vinegar. The result would invariably be me and my brother sitting in his lap while we plundered his meal.

It would be gratifying to report that my parents' combined culinary skills triggered an eating revolution among their discerning Merthyr public. They had the materials. Every month or so a big van would call from an Italian wholesaler in Cardiff to deliver a cornucopia of foodstuffs which are now a commonplace of supermarket shelves, but which were then as rare as caviar. There was every type of pasta, Arborio rice, Parmesan cheese, dried mushrooms, salamis, cooking sausages, Parma ham, huge tins of olive oil and tomato pureé. But while their children often ate like gourmets, their customers turned up their noses at new experiences. As far as they were concerned, olive oil was a nasty medicine you bought at the chemists and garlic the poison that gave the smelly foreigner his rancid breath. I remember the howls of complaint as I packed down in school rugby scrums the day after one of my parents' wonderful meals. "Who's been eating bloody garlic?" Now it would be impossible to find a scrum which did not stink of garlic.

The height of culinary ecstasy for our customers then was the hallmark of the Valleys Italian café, the hot steamed steak and kidney pies. To create these wonders we had to desecrate with misuse one of the outstanding achievements of twentieth century Italian design, the huge silver coffee machines that decorated most Italian cafés in South Wales. These tall, elegant works of art, each topped by a trade-mark eagle with wings outspread as if it was about to take off, sprouted a complex pattern of pipes and valves. Some pipes were designed to

deliver thick gobs of espresso coffee into little cups. Another carried
hot water from the machine's boiler. Some spewed out steam to froth
up the milk for café lattes or cappuccinos. Instead we used the steam
to heat pies wrapped in a thick, podgy dough. They were placed in a
specially designed tin with a hole drilled in its hinged lid. The pipe
passed through the hole and into the pie. After a minute or so you
turned the gooey mess on to a plate.

I have to say I was never a fan. I much preferred the more delicate,
better-made, tastier steak and kidney pie turned out by the father of
my schoolfriends Stan and Peter Thomas. Those pies, warmed in
special heaters, provided the foundation for the Thomas family
fortune. Even serving up their stodgy rivals first thing in the morning
would turn my stomach. But for enthusiasts they were a pleasure
bordering on addiction.

Our small café in a Penydarren, caught between more fashionable
Merthyr and the bigger Dowlais, never made our fortunes. But it did,
as a clear-eyed fellow Italian once pointed out to me, provide a family
of six with a decent living and gave two of us children very good
educations. Keeping it open from 7.30 in the morning until 11 at night
required a collective family effort. My two elder sisters exercised
valuable skills such as making our ice-cream, prized throughout
Merthyr, or dressing the huge window, groaning with jars of sweets
and chocolates, that fronted the café and drew in the customers

Every Saturday, and an occasional Sunday, from the time we were
eleven or twelve my brother and I would give my father a break by
taking our ice-cream van with its driver on to the streets. We alternated morning and afternoon shifts according to where and when we
were due to play rugby for our grammar schools. When my mother
took over in the café on Tuesdays and Thursday evenings to give my
sisters much needed time off, we would go behind the counter for an
hour to give her a break.

My mother would move to the other side of the counter and sit
next to the big coal fire. Her English was far from flawless. She invariably spoke Italian with my brother and me. But that did not prevent
her from holding lively conversations with the friends – wives,
mothers and grandmothers from the surrounding streets – who came
to join her for a cup of tea and a gossip. In such moments the café
become a community focal point where people met to joke, laugh,
chat through their problems and make their difficult lives a little easier.

## HOWARD WINSTONE

The only time I saw the finest boxer Merthyr, perhaps Britain, has produced fight live in the professional ring I was wearing a white jacket and carried a large white tray suspended halter-like from my neck by a leather strap. It was August 1960, and my father had won the concession to sell refreshments at a boxing tournament in the impressive Aberdare Football Stadium, ten miles across the mountain from Merthyr. I was in the Sixth Form and had been urgently summoned from a holiday with relatives in the Rhondda to take part in this significant new departure for the Basinis.

It was not one of my father's more impressive business decisions. We shared the concession with another Merthyr family, the Thomases. They were selling their pies and pasties, and they did a roaring trade among fans whose appetites had been sharpened by alcohol and the scent of blood. My brother and I, on the other hand, were selling ice-cream and chocolate, delicacies which, while they might have tempted lovers packed in the backrow of Merthyr's Castle Cinema, held little attraction for fans whose taste buds had been dulled by beer. I remember forlornly watching my choc ices and ice lollies melt into a gooey mess while my old schoolfriends Stanley and Peter Thomas rushed around the stands emptying tray after tray. At least I had plenty of time to watch the boxing.

If the supporting contests between lumbering heavyweights had more in common with what happens on a butcher's slab than in a sporting stadium, the main bout showed why, at its best, boxing could approach an art form. It featured Howard Winstone, the feather-

weight weighing nine stone, whose mesmerically quick hands and feet created patterns of movement as intricate as Nureyev's. He had famously lost the tips of three fingers on his right hand in an accident as a seventeen year-old operating a metal press in a Merthyr toy factory. If that handicap limited his punching power, it offered little consolation to his opponents. He won almost half his sixty-one victories well

within the scheduled end of the bout by dazzling his challengers into submission. Faced with his overwhelming skills they were demoralised into defeat.

Later, on his way to becoming world champion, he would meet one opponent whose skills more closely matched his own and who had greater physical resources – the Mexican Vincente Saldivar against whom Howard fought and lost three epic battles for the world title. Those bouts would reveal assets to complement his bewitching talent – his fitness, his dedication to his sport, above all, his boundless courage.

Howard was a friend and neighbour as well as a hero. He had been born and brought up in a small terraced house on Penydarren High Street, a quarter of a mile from our café, at a point where the Street began to climb towards Dowlais. His father, Howard senior, was a short, dark, intensely handsome man who embodied Merthyr's rich racial mix; part English, part Welsh, part Irish, part Jewish. For years he had been a costermonger, selling fruit and vegetables from the back of his horse and cart. Despite the crippling wounds he suffered during World War II his manners were as old-world as his vehicle. I remember his courtesy when he called into the café to buy sweets or tobacco. He was a man of impressive dignity.

His wife, Katie, may have shared her husband's Mediterranean looks but she was a very different personality, louder, stronger, more abrasive. They were qualities she would have to call on when her husband died at forty-eight and she was left to bring up her four children. She was fiercely protective, especially of her most talented son. At the end of Winstone's long, destructive bouts with Vicente Saldivar for the world championship, she would be first into the ring to wipe away the tears as well as the blood from a cut eye or mouth. And she was the first to share his delight when he won the world title he richly deserved by beating the Japanese, Mitsunori Seki, in London in 1968.

Howard had inherited his father's dark good looks. He was handsome in an Italianate way, cascades of cherubic curls topping his large blue eyes and delicate mouth. Even in his sixties, rapidly approaching death, the urchin grin was rarely off that face. As a boy he had an irrepressible sense of mischief. On Saturday evenings, having made a few coppers selling *Football Echoes*, he and his mate would call into our café for a hot steak and kidney pie and Oxo beef tea. My mother was often behind the counter, large and powerful but, they estimated, too slow and cumbersome to offer a threat. So they would play games with her, pretending to steal sweets from the counter and making fun of her less than perfect English.

Then came the evening when Howard, brimming confidence, literally overreached himself. As he danced into range, she suddenly flashed out an arm cross the counter and caught him flush on the chin. "It was," he told me decades later, ruefully rubbing that chin, "the hardest left hook I ever took."

Even before he became a professional, his absorption in the sport and its traditions was total. Mindful of Merthyr's history of great mountain fighters and eager to pass his passion and pride in the sport on to the rest of us, he would march us off to the top of the three-hundred foot high slag tips that dominated Penydarren. He would organise his own tournaments, using a pair of old boxing gloves oozing their stuffing and coats for ring posts. Having paired us off, roughly matched for age and weight, he would referee as we tried to knock each other into the middle of the ensuing week. I remember squaring up to my friend Mansel Aylward under Howard's watchful eye. Sadly for Howard, neither of us had been convinced by his eloquence about the dignity of the noble art. We circled each other warily, flurried a few badly aimed punches and collapsed into each other's arms.

Howard's tragedy was that his pride in his accomplishments, his unshakeable faith in himself and his talents drained from him as soon as he retired. Outside the ring, he became as indecisive and uncertain as he had been strong and self-confident in it. As his career was approaching its pinnacle, his private life was marred by scandal and acrimony. His wife Benita, the mother of his four children, ran off with an English construction worker she had met in a Merthyr pub. After he had retired, a succession of businesses he set up failed. A period as a publican proved disastrous, triggering the heavy drinking that would be a feature of his later life. When the money he had earned from boxing disappeared he took a series of jobs, such as a hospital porter and as an executive of a double glazing company. They never lasted more than a month or two.

He never lost his warmth, his sense of humour or his generosity. Sustained by a devoted second wife, Bronwen, with whom he had a son, remembered with affection and respect by the boxing world, revered as a hero by most in his home town, he had a great deal to live for. When you met him in the street or at his neat, immaculately kept home in Merthyr, that urchin grin would quickly light up a face which bore few reminders of his sixty-seven fights. But the eyes that had once brimmed with a delight in life were empty, their light extinguished, it seemed to me, the moment he had walked away from the one thing that had given him a sense of purpose and self-pride. Even as a champion he exuded an icy isolation, cut off by his success from the friends he had grown up with. In his later years it seemed that no amount of love or respect could penetrate the carapace of his loneliness.

All of Merthyr was devastated, but few of us were surprised, when he died in 2000 aged just 61. The love and affection poured out to him by his home town and a grateful nation solidified into the statue, paid for by public subscription, which stands in the St Tydfil's shopping centre in the centre of Merthyr. Showing him seated, bearing the two Lonsdale Belts he won for defending his British Featherweight title, it is a decent work of art. But it does nothing to convey the grace, the power and the beauty this small, slight man from a terraced house in Penydarren brought to his often brutish sport.

## THE LUKEY

The huge gallery of what had once been 'The Lukey', the Lucania Snooker Hall, hung over the pavement like the broad backside of a galleon. Any moment now, you felt, its wood and glass superstructure would collapse into Penydarren High Street below. Instead of the clack of colliding snooker balls, it was the staccato rhythm of men skipping on wooden floorboards that greeted you as you climbed the rickety stairs to the first floor hall. The boxing gym it had become possessed the no-frills realism of black-and white Hollywood movies. Around the ring dominating the room hung a variety of punchbags. Medicine balls and skipping ropes littered the floor. An ancient clock on a peeling wall timed the aspiring champions' training sessions. The toilets smelled, the showers leaked.

A trainer, his waist thickening with age, bustled around the gym in his white shirt sleeves and braces. He wielded a sponge and a bucket of water on which ice formed in winter. A small army of profession-als and eager volunteers helped to condition the battery of aspiring professionals, who sparred and sweated and grimaced with pain as they pounded the punchbags, or braced themselves for the impact of heavy medicine balls thudding into their stomachs. In a corner, absorbing every detail, stood a tall man whose face, dominated by laughing blue eyes, was often black with the coal dust he had worked in all day.

Eddie Thomas, miner turned boxing champion and coal owner, was in the middle of yet another career, this time as the trainer, manager and promoter of fighters like himself. It was the job he did best, one which earned him a unique place in boxing history. Inspired by his passion for the sport, the club based in this decaying hall in one of the oldest, most deprived parts of Merthyr, would become perhaps the best boxing stable in Britain, producing a string of champions. Two of them in the space of a few years would become world title holders. The club's reputation during its heyday in the 1960s would spread around the world. Talented boxers would flock here from all over Britain to train.

Eddie had been the first of those post World War II champions who won Merthyr an unrivalled reputation in the sport. He was the first of the town's three great boxers to be given that most visible and extravagant public accolade, a statue erected in his name. He was born in Colliers Row near Heolgerrig in the south of Merthyr in 1926, the son of a miner. Eddie and his five brothers followed their father underground. They would eventually run their own mines. Four of the five would also become well-known boxing champions. As a youth, Eddie divided his leisure time between boxing and his other great love, singing. He was second tenor in the choir of his local Cyfarthfa Church. The two passions would dovetail when in 1949 he fought Henry Hall for the British welterweight championship at Harringay Arena in London.

By then he had become the darling of a Merthyr Tydfil hungry for entertainment, self-belief and reassurance in the drab days of scarcity and rationing that followed World War II. The town held its breath as entire families huddled around their radios to listen to the commentary on the tense, fifteen-round battle against Hall. Eddie topped his victory by grabbing the ring announcer's microphone and serenading the listening millions with 'Bless This House'. Then Merthyr poured into its streets to celebrate. He went on to win the Empire and European titles before he retired in 1954. It was the start of his most productive career.

A man with a strong sense of pride in his home town and of civic duty, he was convinced that boxing could give those from Merthyr's poverty-stricken streets a sense of discipline, a purpose in life and a chance to win financial security for themselves and their families. His drive to help young men with talent stemmed perhaps in part from his own struggles against neglect and exploitation as a young boxer. He regularly came straight from a shift down the mine to travel to a

contest. Tall for a welterweight, he faced agonising battles to make the weight for his bouts. His strength-sapping attempts to sweat off a few ounces included sitting in front of a roaring fire wearing several overcoats for hours before a fight. He suffered with brittle bones in his hands and toward the end of his career he was routinely given painkilling injections before entering the ring.

He opened gyms in two public houses in Dowlais before moving to the disused snooker hall in Penydarren. The stable's first major success came with the arrival of slight youth who happened to live just a few doors from the new gym. Howard Winstone had once been a delivery boy in the Co-op store opposite the gym. He had already proved his talent by winning a gold medal at the 1956 Empire Games in Cardiff. Now, under Eddie Thomas's guidance, he forged the professional career that would eventually earn him a world title.

The relationship between Eddie and his most famous protégé has been compared to that between father and son. The manager's belief in the unmatched skills of his pupil and his ability to bring the young featherweight to a peak of fitness for each bout clearly played a crucial, perhaps the crucial, part in Howard's success. But like a father and son, the relationship was sometimes marred by festering quarrels.

The boxers based at the gym came in all shapes, sizes and levels of achievement; heavyweights like Carl Gizzi and Malcolm Price; brilliant light heavyweights like Eddie Avoth, middleweights such as John Gamble. Some, like Dai Gardiner, went on to become successful managers themselves. The stable's most successful champion after Winstone was the Scot, Ken Buchanan. A brilliant boxer-fighter, Buchanan would win the world lightweight title. He, too, quarrelled with Eddie because he believed he was not earning the sort of money he deserved. But after they parted, the Scot never repeated the success he enjoyed with the Merthyr manager.

Often, after their training sessions, Eddie and his boxers would leave the gym and stroll two-hundred yards down the road for coffee and sandwiches in my father's café. With their sharp Italian suits they exuded a sense of well-being and prosperity the rest of us envied. Their lifestyles made them heroes in a Merthyr where most aspired to a lifetime in a factory or on the dole. They bantered with each other, flirted with my elder sisters. But they were impeccably behaved.

When the demolition of Penydarren High Street finally put paid to the gym in the early Seventies, Eddie continued to encourage and advise young boxers. Some travelled to stay with him and his wife, Kay, in their impressive detached home next to the Penydarren Park football ground. But he poured more and more of his energies into his business and into the running of his home town. Backed by the determined, forceful, loyal Kay, he became an Independent councillor and frequent thorn in the side of the town's Labour-controlled council. He battled to improve the standard of council housing in Merthyr. He and Kay campaigned for years against the slum-like conditions in the high-rise Dowlais Flats, built in the Sixties but plagued by problems like widespread damp. Eventually, they were demolished.

However hard he fought for his boxers and for his town, Eddie never lost his reputation as one of Nature's gentlemen. He retained his reputation for honesty, compassion and dignity tempered with a strong sensed of fun, right up to his death from cancer in 1997, aged seventy. When calls to ban boxing crescendoed because several high profile boxers died or were crippled by injuries sustained during bouts, he remained unshakably committed to the sport. He explained to me patiently that the instinct to fight was part of human nature. You could not eradicate it. You could harness it, civilise it, make it a force for good in a young man's life. You might question his beliefs. You could never doubt his sincerity.

When Merthyr and Wales raised money for a statue to preserve his memory, the council refused to allow it to stand outside the new Civic Centre. Whatever the motivation, it was an inspired decision. Instead, the statue was erected in the memorial garden that occupies the spot where Bethesda Chapel had once stood. One of Eddie's great heroes, Joseph Parry, first learned to love music attending Bethesda as a child. Knowing that he shares the spot with the shade of Merthyr's – and Wales's – greatest composer would surely delight the boxer who loved to serenade his fans with a song.

## CYFARTHFA CASTLE GRAMMAR SCHOOL

It was the ideal setting in which to study Alphonse de Lamartine, the great French poet of romantic love and nature: sitting on the edge of a lush green lawn, the size of several rugby pitches, which swept down to a swan-flecked boating lake. Beyond marched the precise and graceful arches of the Cefn railway viaduct, grey-white against the wooded hillside. To the left of the lawn, canopied by clusters of spreading horse chestnuts, more trees formed an elegant avenue down which the long drive wound to distant park gates guarded by an ancient limestone lodge. Behind us and to our right, acres of woodland rose gently to the top of the ridge. Immediately behind us, as we recited Lamartine to each other in the summer sunshine, stood the majestic, castellated mock castle in 160 acres of parkland with fountains, manicured gardens, hothouses, bandstands, bowling greens, tennis courts, ruined ice houses and endless woodland walks. As we studied 'Le Lac', Lamartine's long cry of longing for his dead lover, I sat across the grass from the girl who, although she did not know it, was the focus of my own fantasy of romantic love.

To go to school in the castle was to pass into a world of privilege the rich would pay thousands of pounds a year to acquire for their children. In the Merthyr of the Fifties and Sixties it was free for the children of some of Europe's worst slums; tightly-packed, overcrowded, noxious nineteenth century courts and alleys which still polluted the centres of Merthyr and Dowlais. Among the gifts Cyfarthfa Castle Grammar School bestowed on us were a sense of space, of freedom, of air untainted by the grime of factory smoke and of a beauty born out of symmetry and order, as we looked out of tall classroom windows on to sculpted bushes and flower beds or stone fountains draped with renaissance cherubs.

The interior of the castle had changed out of recognition in the fifty years since the ironmasters, the Crawshays, had moved out and the school had moved in. Tall-ceilinged bedrooms, offices and servants'

quarters had become classrooms filled with graffiti-carved desks and blackboards or science labs bristling with bunsen burners. Changing rooms and showers had been added, fields converted into soccer, hockey or rugby pitches. Quadrangles and terraces had become car parks and playgrounds. Only a handful of the richly decorated state rooms, drawing rooms, libraries and music rooms remained to illustrate the opulence of life in the castle during the Crawshay years. They had been turned into a museum and art gallery. But a hint of its former glory remained in the part of the castle we occupied. Our tall and spacious assembly halls, downstairs for the boys, upstairs for the girls, retained the highly-polished, sprung wooden floors of the ballrooms they once were. Richly coloured Victorian tiles decorated our classroom walls. We clattered past stained glass windows and down staircases which had once echoed to the tread of the Crawshays' guests there, like Charles Darwin or the poet Robert Browning.

The school was, in the words of one of its best-known products, the historian Sir Glanmor Williams, a goodish Welsh grammar school; some were better, many worse. The standard of teaching varied enormously, from the indifferent and the incompetent to the conscientious and the caring. Our education was, after 'O' levels, rigidly compartmentalised and unforgivably indifferent to Merthyr's rich historical and cultural background. At the start of the sixth form I wanted to combine traditional arts subjects like history and English with the science of chemistry for 'A' levels. Today no-one would bat an eyelid. Then my wish was met with the shocked disapproval that greeted Oliver Twist's request for more. I was told to stick to the arts and take French. I remember having only one lesson on Merthyr's

unique history in my seven years at the school. It was part of my sixth form history course and highlighted what was believed to be Wales's first dissenting chapel, situated to the south west of Merthyr. Fired with enthusiasm, my friend Roger Howell, like me the son of a small businessman who had a grocer's shop fifty yards from my father's café, and I strode out to find what was left of it. We walked as far as Georgetown, within a mile or so of the chapel ruins, when we met a merchant seaman from our village of Penydarren and fell into the nearest pub, appropriately named The Ship. We spent the afternoon there before staggering home. It would be another forty years before I finally got to see what remained of that chapel.

My most important lessons at Cyfarthfa were learned outside the classroom. In our first year we were given the absurd choice of either Welsh or French as our 'foreign' language. Most, including me, opted for French on the hopelessly wrong assumption that it would be the most useful to us in later life. So I was never taught by Havard Walters, the straight-backed, demanding, scrupulously fair Welsh master who summed up most of what was best about Cyfarthfa. He did supervise some of our free periods. I remember during one of those in our second or third year him calling me to his desk.

"Do you speak Italian?"

My mother, whose grasp of English remained shaky more than thirty years after she had arrived in Wales, almost invariably spoke to me in her Italian dialect of which I understood every word. But I replied to her in English.

I looked down at my feet and shuffled with embarrassment.

"No sir."

"You damn well should" he growled. "It's your birthright."

In that brief moment he taught me the life-shaping lesson that caring for your own roots and culture is the first necessary step to caring for the rest of humanity. Years later I began the slow process of mastering Italian.

Outside the classroom we debated, we acted – something I loved – and, of course, played sport. Until I arrived at Cyfarthfa, my first love had been soccer and in my first year I went with friends to watch Cardiff City play in the First Division against sides like Arsenal and Manchester United, when crowds of 40,000 were commonplace. Like the football hooligans we might have become, we did our best to trash the trains in which we travelled to Ninian Park. Luckily, perhaps, for my soul and my potentially criminal future, Cyfarthfa quickly taught me to love rugby. I can still remember the stomach-churning excitement, the sheer joy, as on a fine September afternoon we trekked up through the woods behind the castle to our steeply-sloping, lung-tearing pitch for the first game of the season.

The richest nourishment for the soul during the seven crucial years I spent at the castle school came from the friends I made there. Some I have not seen since. Some have died in tragic circumstances;

as alcoholics, suicides, two as the victims of murder. Elliot Fine, tall, broad-shouldered, loud, charismatic, was a gifted athlete and a good friend despite the fact he was several years older than me. Warm, frank, engaging, a devoted family man, Elliot was tragically stabbed in an anti-Semitic attack on his way to his synagogue in Cardiff one Saturday in 1981.

Some have remained close during the 45 years since we left the school; men like Professor Mansel Aylward, doctor, pioneering scientist, government adviser, academic. I have known and loved his wife, Angela, for almost as long as he has – they began their relationship in our third year at Cyfarthfa. Friends like Darya Francis and Peter Phillips, another immigrant, an Englishman who first came to Merthyr with his parents because his father was a senior executive at the Hoover Washing Machine factory. Peter, the quintessential Englishman, with a taste for bow ties, real beer and the English countryside, yet for decades more devoted to Merthyr than any of us; more emotional, more sentimental than the reputedly passionate Welshmen and Italians among whom he grew up.

And there were Stan and Peter, the Thomas brothers, brought up, like my brother and I, in the family business. Like me, they were passionate about Merthyr and rugby, organising their own matches on the pitch next to their father's pie factory in Rhydycar, south of Merthyr. We would change in the factory. Stan, the elder, loved boxing and became a schoolboy champion. Unlike me, they went into the family business when they left Cyfarthfa. Unlike me, they became entrepreneurs and property developers, each year figuring high in Britain's Rich List. Both have retained their strong ties with the town, maintaining the friendships they developed during their childhood. Both are major benefactors of Wales as well as Merthyr, as generous charity donors and organisers. Stan, now Sir Stanley, patron of so many organisations in Wales as well as in his home town, richly deserved the Freedom of the Merthyr Borough bestowed on him in 2000. Eight years previously, the honour had been given to his father, Stanley senior.

If the school broadened my intellectual horizons, those friends hastened my emotional maturity. They taught me to value honesty, loyalty and trust as well as laughter; to cherish myself and my abilities; to reach out to the world, in Browning's words, "Ah, but a man's reach should exceed his grasp, Or what's a heaven for?" Our debates and arguments opened up thrilling new emotional and intellectual possibilities. The friendships I made there are Cyfarthfa's true legacy.

## TREVITHICK TRADING ESTATE

It is one of those small trading estates that fill nooks and crannies all over the Valleys, as if their mere presence will magically conjure up enterprise, imagination and jobs. The name board on the first of its three large units this mild, overcast afternoon in spring, reads Woodies Furniture. It is locked and silent. On the building opposite hangs a sign familiar on any of the Valleys industrial estates: To Let. In the corner, the third unit adds a touch of the exotic to a drab corner of Penydarren. It is, it proclaims in bold letters, the home of Master Brew which imports coffee from Nairobi. A brief chat on the doorstep to the man I take to be the owner reveals the company also imports and sells coffee-making machinery. Over his shoulder I spot a cabinet displaying a tantalising array of the addict's paraphernalia – percolators, filters, plungers. Behind his unit stands a lorry belonging to the Welcome School of Motoring which specialises in training heavy goods drivers. Its presence here has a symbolic resonance. In the estate's opposite corner, next to the entrance guarded by two ferocious dogs mercifully imprisoned behind a wire fence, is a modest, single-storey transport café. With what I take to be an admirable sense of self-mockery, a board outside its door announces branches in New York, Paris and Stockholm.

It is a meagre harvest for a site on which was born the technology which ushered in a new world. In this hollow, fifty feet below Penydarren High Street, less than 150 years ago stood one of the four great works that made Merthyr the world's biggest centre for the manufacture of iron and the crucible of the Industrial Revolution. The Penydarren Works may have been the last and the smallest of Merthyr's giants, but in its heyday it employed more than 1500 people and its products, valued for their quality, travelled all over the world. In 1830, forty-six years after it opened, it supplied the rails for the Liverpool and Manchester, the world's first railway to link two major towns. On those rails ran George Stephenson's Rocket, a

richly ironic moment in railway history.

A painting of the Penydarren Ironworks at the turn of the nineteenth century shows why the satanic beauty of these early works attracted awe-struck artists by the carriageful. In the left hand corner as you look south towards Merthyr a row of tall, grim blast furnaces stand flush against the hillside, their flues breathing tongues of flame. They are topped by a row of calcinating kilns, each as small and as dark as a hermit's cell. Here iron ore was roasted before it was fed into the mouths of the furnaces. Below, fronting the massive, oblong furnaces and dwarfed by them, gather a group of brick buildings, each with a sloping roof and three arched entrances. They are the casting houses where molten iron, just tapped from the bottom of the furnaces, is allowed to cool in beds, or 'pigs', of sand.

Three tall, pencil-slim chimneys rise into the smoke-filled air from forges and engine houses supplying the blast to the furnaces. Further down the little valley more fires glow from forges and rolling mills from which sprout more thin chimneys like antennae. Tramroads, some travelling south to Merthyr and beyond, others turning north to the limestone quarries of Morlais, web the scene. Between them, skirting the works, runs the polluted Morlais Brook. Above, Penydarren High Street is busy with people and horse-drawn carts.

For much of its short life – it closed in 1859 – the Penydarren works was run by Samuel Homfray, the Staffordshire ironmaster who epitomised the faults and virtues of the pioneering breed. A bull-necked, bull-headed man he was, said his contemporaries, foul-mouthed and at the mercy of his unbridled passions. A circuit judge, used to the judicious language of his courts, described his "obstinacy of temper and a roughness of manners". He was, the judge said, "a very dangerous person for those who are connected with him and for others". Even the choleric Richard Crawshay, whose own rudeness was legendary, called him "so Ungratefull and Litigious that I cannot be on neighbourly terms with him." Whatever his faults, Homfray was a man of vision with the entrepreneur's keen eye for the innovative in technology and for the money-making talents of others. And he had the courage to back his judgement. When in 1803 he heard of a Cornish engineer who was revolutionising the design of engines by the use of high pressure steam, Homfray travelled to meet the prodigy then working at Abraham Darby's ironworks in Coalbrookdale, Shropshire. The Penydarren magnate soon persuaded Richard Trevithick, aged thirty-two, down to South Wales to work for him.

The plan was for Trevithick to build a stationary engine to drive a steam hammer at Penydarren. But the engineer was excited by the possibilities offered by the nine and a half mile tramroad which ran from Penydarren to meet the Glamorgan Canal at Abercynon. The canal had been the Merthyr ironmasters' solution to the problem of how to get their products down to the port of Cardiff and on to their customers without having to use roads which were little better than cart tracks. The waterway had been financed by all four of the Merthyr ironworks and was a major engineering feat. No less than forty-nine locks were needed to negotiate the twenty-four miles and the six-hundred foot drop between Merthyr and Cardiff. But almost a soon as it was opened in 1794 it became congested. Horse-drawn barges piled with iron queued for days for the chance to use it. The canal began at Crawshay's Cyfarthfa works and he was its main shareholder. When he insisted his products should have priority, his resentful rivals retaliated by building the tramroad which bypassed the congested upper reaches of the canal.

Trevithick, who had already adapted his high pressure steam engines to travel on roads, now rose to the challenge presented by the tramroad which, like the canal, relied on horsepower to draw its trams. The engineer, with a temperament as mercurial as that of his new employer, modified his Penydarren engine so that it could replace the horses. Homfray's Merthyr rivals poured scorn on the proposal. Predictably, Richard Crawshay, labelled Merthyr's tyranni- cal 'Moloch the Iron King' by a contemporary, was particularly scathing when he saw the engine. Outraged at the attacks on his protégé, Homfray demanded Crawshay should put his money where his mouth was. He proposed a wager for the enormous sum of five-hundred guineas on whether the locomotive could haul ten tons of iron the nine and a half miles to Abercynon. Crawshay accepted.

## PENYDARREN TO THE CANAL – TREVITHICK'S JOURNEY

The journey dazzles with the excitement and expectation of a carni- val parade. The primitive engine with its black, barrel-like boiler, huge flywheel and protruding levers resembles a Heath Robinson nightmare as it pulls its five tram wagons carrying ten tons of iron down a set of rails 4ft 4ins apart. Its overall load is perhaps two and a half times that since around seventy of the cheering crowds through which it has trundled on its way through Merthyr and the Taff Valley have clambered onto the wagons determined to catch a free ride. They cheer and wave their hats and scarves as the engine, its tall chimney belching fire and black smoke, confidently gathers pace on the flat. They howl with derision as it slows on the inclines and tremble with fear as it quickens downhill, threatening to derail and throw them all into the street or bushes or down a muddy embankment. Scores more follow, some on horseback, some scrambling to keep up with the engine's sedate 5mph. Their numbers swell as all down the route onlookers, attracted by the noise and the smoke and the flames, rush for their place in history.

In front of the engine marches a huge man, well over 6ft tall, whose stride easily outpaces the monster at his back. His barrel-chested physique confirms his reputation for prodigious strength. He can, his friends witness, lift weights of half a ton and throw a sledge hammer soaring over a tall engine house. The stick he carries twitches with tension as he listens for the noises that indicate the engine is about to breakdown or even explode, sending it and almost certainly him to kingdom come.

The big man was Richard Trevithick, a Cornish engineer who in his comparatively short career had revolutionised the design of the steam engine, mired himself in controversy and earned the undying enmity of James Watt, the most famous engineer of his day. Trevithick, the son of a Cornish tin mine 'captain', or manager, had himself learned his engineer skills working the mines of his native land. He had put those skills to good use creating the high pressure steam engine which not only allowed him to produce more efficient stationary devices, able to drive the heaviest, most complex machinery, but also enabled him to create engines which could travel on roads and, as he was proving this cold, late winter morning in Merthyr, haul loads on rails.

The inventor of the steam engine, James Watt, and his partner Matthew Boulton, alarmed that the brash, driven, newcomer was about to ruin their lucrative monopoly, launched a vociferous publicity campaign against Trevithick and his machine. It was dangerous and he should be hanged! Watt thundered. Their cause was boosted when in 1803, one of Trevithick's stationary engines at Greenwich in London, exploded, killing three people. The accident had been entirely due to the negligence of the worker responsible for its maintenance, a fact Watt and Boulton conveniently ignored.

That historic first journey by rail for a steam locomotive on February 21, 1804 was deemed a success, despite the interruptions needed to clear stones from the track and to cut down overhanging trees. The nine and a half miles from the Penydarren Ironworks to the Glamorgan Canal at Abercynon was completed in little more than four hours. Not even the fact that the engine broke down on the return journey could temper the satisfaction of Trevithick and his backer, Samuel Homfray, the owner of the Penydarren works.

But their triumph proved to be as ephemeral as their engine's billowing smoke. The immediate problem was one that would plague the new mode of transport for decades: the brittle iron rails over which Trevithick's machine travelled cracked and disintegrated under its weight. Nor would Homfray's 500 guinea wager with his rival ironmaster rival Richard Crawshay be paid. The owner of a third Merthyr works, Richard Hill, had been given the money to adjudicate the bet. Hill, who ran the Plymouth works south of the town, refused to hand it over because part of the track running through a tunnel had to be relaid to accommodate the engine. That made the bet invalid, Hill claimed, because the engine had not travelled over the tramroad as precisely stipulated in the wager. The journey was repeated at least

four times in the coming months. But there is no evidence the fastidious Hill ever paid the abrasive and unpopular Homfray. Trevithick and his paymaster abandoned their experiments with railway travel and the engine reverted to its original role of driving a steam hammer at the Penydarren Works.

If the disintegrating rails were the immediate cause of the abandonment, there might

have been important underlying factors. It was the time of the massive expansion of canals as the main method of transport for the dawning Industrial Revolution. Rail travel was seen as a novelty and a sideshow. For all their gifts, neither Trevithick nor Homfrey grasped the full potential of railways, which would within fifty years transform Victorian Britain and provide the efficient system of transport needed for the

creation of industrial and urban civilisation across the globe.

Trevithick himself suffered from what tabloid psychologists would regard as the besetting sin of restless genius. Passionately interested in ideas as opposed to making money, he lacked the motivation needed to pursue a single goal to its conclusion. Fresh challenges always arrived to divert his attention. It was left to others, like the father and son team of George and Robert Stephenson, to profit from the Cornishman's pioneering work and create the commercially viable locomotives which ran on the first railways like the Stockton and Darlington and the Liverpool and Manchester. By the time the latter opened in 1830 Trevithick had long since sold his patent on his locomotive and, after many years in South America, fruitlessly chasing commercial success, was back in Britain penniless. In his lifetime critics queued to condemn the way he had wasted his enormous talents, a cry taken up by succeeding generations.

His answer showed the generosity of his spirit. A few months before his death in 1833, aged 62, he wrote to a friend. "I have been branded with folly and madness for attempting what the world calls impossibilities…. This so far has been my reward from the public; but should this be all, I shall be satisfied by the great secret pleasure and laudable pride that I feel in my own breast from having been the instrument of bringing forward and maturing new principles and new arrangements of boundless value to my country.

"However much I may be straitened in pecuniary circumstances, the great honour of being a useful subject can ever be taken from me, which to me far exceeds riches."

When Stephenson's famous engine, The Rocket, ushered in the

railway era on the Liverpool and Manchester line in 1830, the rails it travelled on had been made at Penydarren.

## THE CANAL

A pair of squabbling moorhens beat the pond-calm water to a frenzy. Trees on the thickly-wooded far bank, that rises steeply to a 60 foot ridge, trail their branches through the water like fingers. A family of mallards glide past on a carpet of water lilies. A chaffinch streaks and chatters through the canopy of leaves. This twelve-hundred yard stretch of water teeming with wildlife – wait and you may see the brilliant blue of a kingfisher burn briefly against the dark trees – is a moment of rural calm preserved in the cacophony of Cardiff. An ugly modern housing estate presses against its western flank. Half a mile to the east cars pour into a superstore. Half a mile beyond that, the M4 bounds westwards on concrete stilts.

But this sliver of the city is anything but a relic from a rural past long since buried under urban sprawl. It is what remains of the wellspring of Cardiff's wealth, the fountainhead of the trade which turned a small and shrinking seaside town into a commercial power-house. This narrow channel dappled by a pale morning sun is the last remaining stretch of the Glamorgan Canal running between Merthyr and Cardiff. Along it flowed the trade which sparked the coastal community's growth from a village of 1800 poor fishermen and craftsmen to the Welsh metropolis, the capital of the country it has spent much of its past deriding. Opened in 1793, the canal was a remarkable feat of engineering with no less than fifty-two locks along the twenty-five and a half miles from its source within the Cyfarthfa Ironworks to its eventual end on the southern tip of the Taff Estuary. The locks were needed to carry the barges down the six-hundred foot drop between a Merthyr about to become the world's most important centre for iron manufacture and a Cardiff still languishing in obscure poverty. The determination with which Merthyr's ironmasters, led by the single-minded Richard Crawshay, tackled this difficult and expensive project reflected how badly they needed it. Having been drawn up the Taff Valley by an abundance of what they needed to make iron-wood, coal, limestone and iron ore – they faced the problem of how to get their products to their customers. At first they were forced to use pack horses, laboriously trekking along the rutted mountain path they had themselves used when they first arrived in

Merthyr. It stretched across the moorland east of Merthyr to Caerphilly before dropping down to Cardiff and the waiting ships. The building of a road along the valley floor, on the route more or less taken by the present A470, eased their problem. But it was the canal that allowed them to expand their trade to the point where it would make them rich beyond their dreams of avarice. While a wagon drawn by four horses could carry two tons of iron to down the road, a canal barge pulled by a single horse would carry twenty-five tons. Soon more than 100,000 tons of iron a year travelled along the canal. And the barges carried more than that in another Merthyr product, one which in the long tem would prove more important to the city than iron – coal. The canal had become the umbilical cord along which nourishment flowed from Merthyr to its sickly infant.

Under the impact of the Merthyr trade, Cardiff began to expand – from around 1,870 inhabitants in 1801 to more than 6,000 by 1831. Wharves and docks were built to handle the iron and coal. Banks, coffee rooms, even a racecourse, were opened to cater for its expanding population. If the city's lightning-fast expansion in the second half of the nineteenth century was triggered by the exploitation of the abundant coal seams of the Rhondda and Cynon Valley, the foundation for that expansion had been laid by the trade with Merthyr.

From the start Cardiff recognised its dependence on Merthyr and the other valley towns. But dependence did not spawn gratitude. The resentful port affected to despise its hillbilly neighbours. The feeling was exacerbated by differences in politics, race and language. While Merthyr, with its strong Unitarian presence, embraced radical, working class politics, Cardiff, a borough founded to service its

Marcher Lord castle, espoused the small 'c' conservatism of the shopkeeper and craftsman. Popular uprisings in Merthyr, such as those of 1816 and 1831, left Cardiff appalled and apprehensive. Merthyr's outrage at the hanging in Cardiff in 1831 of the innocent Dic Penderyn contrasted starkly with the latter's relief that the execution had passed off peacefully. Medieval Cardiff, perceptably English, frequently found itself at war with the Welsh-speaking princes to the north. The racial differences persisted. In 1881, thirty per cent of Cardiff's population was English-born. The vast majority of the migrants who had flooded into Welsh-speaking Merthyr, in the first half of the century, came from other parts of Wales. The town remained a stronghold of Welsh language culture and journalism throughout the nineteenth century. The differences continue. In the 1997 referendum, Cardiff rejected the pleas for self-government by the country of which it is happy to call itself the capital by a massive 55.6 per cent to 44.4 per cent. Merthyr voted for a Welsh Assembly by the even more emphatic 58.2 per cent to 41.8 per cent.

The establishment of a second Dowlais Steelworks, on Cardiff's bleak East Moors shore in 1891, was the most obvious sign of how radically the economic roles of the two communities had changed. The works, at first intended to supplement its Merthyr parent, soon took over. Within forty years the original Dowlais works had closed, plunging its community and the rest of Merthyr into deep depression. The Valleys town, once so dominant, had become Cardiff's reliant junior. Now the city and its M4 corridor offer Merthyr people the best chance of local employment. Much of the town is becoming Cardiff's dormitory, offering cheaper housing to those who work in the city. The intense rivalry spawned by professional soccer sides of equal ability has long since subsided into acceptance of Cardiff's dominance. Merthyr, which has recently lacked even a cinema, now looks to Cardiff for entertainment, excitement and for lessons in some of the finer things of life. Merthyr's parental concern for its sickly offspring has become affection and admiration for a city which offers so much.

My own first memories of Cardiff remain vivid: the excitement I felt as a toddler, eating with my younger brother off the crisp white tablecloths of the vast New Continental Restaurant, where the Capitol shopping precinct now stands, while the owner, Mrs Carpanini, came to chat to our parents; learning to love the theatre in pantos at the New Theatre; as a fourteen year-old sneaking a half pint of beer in the Alexandra Hotel before dashing off, hooting with excitement, to an international rugby match at the Cardiff Arms Park. For a proud son of perhaps the most fascinating town in Wales, living on the doorstep of a big city, even one as snootily condescending as Cardiff, offered its compensations.

## PENYDARREN PARK

The players flicker like figures in a silent film in the misty, gaslight glow of the floodlights. They howl like banshees at each other, their cacophony drowning the noise from a crowd of perhaps three-hundred dotted around the ground. "Up your arse!" screams a home team player to a colleague about to be tackled from behind. A lone, infuriated fan responds with a burst of scatter-gun insults aimed at the referee, his assistants, the opposing team, the home side. "Deaf as well as blind are 'ew, ref?" "Offside? Never! Fuck off to Specsavers!" "It's like watching the Chuckle Brothers!" A group of three or four fans gathered on the covered terraces to my right stir from their lethargy long enough to bawl a chorus of what is presumably "Come on You Tyds" – short for "Tydfilians." It comes out as "Come on You Turds". The game limps inexorably to a 0-0 draw.

These days, supporting Merthyr Tydfil AFC in the English Southern League Premier Division has more in common with a desultory church gathering than with a major sporting event. The few remaining fans are the remnants of generations of supporters, to whom a trip to Penydarren Park was a compelling highlight of their lives. Their successors are motivated more by habit and a vague sense of duty than by the expectation of passion and success that drew their fathers and grandfathers.

In the years following World War II, crowds of between 5,000 and 10,000 flocked here to watch a Merthyr side with the faintly patronising label of the best outside the Football League. It was stuffed with rejects from that league. For a number their best days, often spent in uniform during World War II, were long behind them. Some had started at Merthyr, moved on to higher things and returned to play out a few stately seasons before retirement. Others came to end careers spent elsewhere. Some of the best, like the cultured half-back Dai Lloyd, or the tricky winger Jenkin Powell, had been content to remain with their home town for most of their playing days. Some were part-timers, publicans, teachers, bricklayers. Others were full-time professionals often earning more than their Football League counterparts. They were, by today's parsimonious standards, prodigiously prolific. Centre forward Trevor Reynolds, successor to the legendary Bill Hullett, hammered in 73 goals in a season. Powell, short, dapper, with a pencil-thin moustache and a mass of black, elegantly coiffured hair, was as immaculately-dressed on the pitch as off. His taste for fastidious grooming did not hinder his effectivness as a footballer. As a winger he scored fifty-three goals in a season. They became heroes in a town starved of entertainment by World War II and beginning to enjoy a new prosperity triggered by the factories making goods that ranged from washing machines to women's lingerie which had replaced coal and steel.

Often, on the ground's northern terrace in the shadow of the elegant, decaying Penydarren House, stood a middle-aged Italian immigrant whose café was a mile up the road. On either side of my father, clinging to his hands, stood my younger brother and I, aged perhaps five and seven, enthralled by the colour and the spectacle. In our dazzled eyes, ageing has-beens were transformed into lithe, spring-heeled gods and Penydarren Park into an Elysian field of happiness. The large, raw-boned Bill Hullett, slightly ridiculous in his black knee-length knickers and baggy white shirt, moved with a slow, absorbed grace. He was a brilliant header of the ball and scored a high proportion of his goals that way. His long head, with its tall forehead and receding waves of black hair, could impart the speed of a bullet to a football. He was big enough and brave enough to shrug off the most dangerous challenges. His wife would ascribe his comparatively early death, at sixty-six, to the brain damage inflicted by constantly heading that heavy leather ball and to the injuries caused by a combination of his bravery and the skulduggery of defenders. Perhaps his greatest tragedy was that he spent what should have been his most productive years as a footballer in the RAF during World War II.

The short, mercurial Jenkin Powell had legs so bowed it was a miracle he could walk, let alone run with an eel's electric speed. He taunted an endless succession of full-backs with mesmerising dribbles before shooting with great power. Journalists and fans usually softened his first name to Shenkin. From there it was short step to the nickname, "Stinkin'". But it was always a term of affection.

However strong the nostalgic glow cast over it by the passage of six decades, you cannot deny that team's quality. It won the Southern League Championship, the most prestigious outside the Football League, four times in five years between 1949 and 1954. It missed the fifth by a point or two. It won two Welsh Cups against Football League opposition from Cardiff, Newport, Swansea and Wrexham. That side, building on the tradition established by its predecessor, Merthyr Town, part of the Third Division for a decade in the 1920s and 1930s, made Merthyr an island of soccer fever in a sea of rugby passion.

The highlight of my own short footballing career was an appearance at hallowed Penydarren Park. A tall and large eleven year-old, I was goalkeeper for St Illtyd's RC Junior School. We normally played on The Bont, which fronted the school, the pitch reclaimed from industrial wasteland. We believed that if you fell and cut yourself on that dirt you would probably contract a terrible disease from which your legs would fall off. That and my size proved powerful deterrents to diving in pursuit of shots to the far corners of my goal. But I was pretty good at fielding those fairly close to me, cutting out crosses and generally dominating my area.

We wore green shirts – not surprising given the Irish background of most of our players – and we were a good side with clever attackers, like Colin 'Bubsy' Mullins, our small, baby-faced, talented captain. We also had a strong defence. In 1954, my last in junior school, we played in the first cup final organised for Merthyr's under 11 soccer sides. As the winners of the league in the northern half of the borough we played our counterparts in the south, Troedyrhiw.

The crowd who watched our match, one fine morning in early May, made up in passion what it lacked in numbers. Among the proud parents was my father, standing as he always did behind the goal at the northern end of the ground. At stake was a massive silver trophy, the Buckland Cup, named after one of the powerful Berry brothers, Seymour, Lord Buckland, coal and steel magnate whose generosity to his home town was legendary.

The vast spaces of the heavily-grassed Penydarren Park were suitably reduced for our young legs. Corner kicks, for example, were taken from the edge of the penalty area. But the goals I defended were the same as those guarded by a string of top-class Merthyr keepers including the great 'Tiger' Reid. The match was a cliff-hanger, not decided until the last minute. Ten minutes into it, according to the watch of the *Merthyr Express* reporter, a Troedyrhiw player called Geoff Davies sent a fierce shot high towards the far right corner of my goal. Uninhibited by my fears of falling on The Bont and aware that my father was watching from behind that goal, I launched into what I imagined was a graceful swallow dive – and missed. It was, as far as I remember, the only shot I was called upon to save during the match. Our dangerous forwards pressed fruitlessly for the equaliser. Then with just thirty seconds to go, the dancing feet of Bubsy Mullins took him past floundering defender after floundering defender before he stroked the ball home. We had equalised! The sides shared the trophy, each holding it for six months. I still have my photograph of our proud team with the cup which all but dwarves little 'Bubsy'.

I should have felt badly about letting in that goal so early in the match. I didn't. Instead, I was suffused by a warm glow of pride because of what I considered my spectacular effort at saving the goal. It was a typical Italian reaction, the belief that making a 'bella figura', cutting a colourful dash, is more important than quiet achievement. It would take a lifetime to learn that unspectacular success is preferable to failure, however valiant or flashy.

## PENYDARREN PARK – RIOTOUS CULTURE

Its position, close to the centre of mountainous Merthyr, makes the plateau on which Penydarren Park is built as valuable as a gold mine. Its location explains why it has played a crucial role in the cultural, social and political, as well as the sporting, history of the town. Almost 2,000 years ago the Romans seized on this island of flat land in a rolling sea of hills as the location for a link in the chain of forts designed to keep the warring Silurian Celts firmly subjugated. The oblong-shaped military camp had streets and shops, a well-stocked granary, baths, living accommodation for up to 1,000 troops and a luxurious home for their commander.

Sixteen hundred years later, the troops would return, this time to put down an uprising by thousands of natives as combative as their Celtic predecessors. In 1831, the ironworkers and miners of a Merthyr mushrooming in size took to the streets to protest over cuts in their wages and their treatment by a local debtors' court and to call for political reform. Their shaken rulers, the ironmasters, their managers and magistrates, barricaded themselves into their homes and called in the troops, which included a detachment of the Argyll and Sutherland Highlanders, as well as the local militia. Their headquarters, for eight long, hot days as the rising ebbed and flowed in late May and early June, was the first of the great mansions built by the town's flamboyant iron entrepreneurs. Penydarren House rose on a ridge in the north east corner of what is now the Penydarren Park football stadium. Built almost fifty years before the rising, it was, with its well proportioned windows and delicately carved doorways and porches, Merthyr's most elegant Georgian building. It was the creation of the most arrogant and ferocious of the ironmasters, Samuel Homfray, owner of the Penydarren Ironworks, whose entrance was just across the road from his new home. But the nightmarish inferno of the works, with its flaming furnaces, its chimneys billowing smoke and its cacophony of men, animals and machinery, could not have been further removed from the Arcadian calm of the house. The Dowlais historian, Gwyn Alf Williams, has left us a glimpse of Penydarren House in its prime during the 1831 revolt. "The grounds were extensive with trees and five park seats. The house had a

large front hall, complete with an organ, a drawing room, library, dining room and dressing room, all with white marble hearths. Upstairs, there were seven bedrooms, four with their own dressing rooms, a schoolroom, governess's room and a maid's workroom; in the attic, five rooms for groom, butler, gardener and housekeeper."

Homfray, the far-sighted backer of railway pioneer Richard Trevithick, basked in this splendid ostentation. When he made the journey of a mile into the heart of Merthyr, he went in a carriage drawn by four horses and manned by footmen resplendent in their scarlet and yellow uniforms. By the time of the 1831 Rising, the families of two other Penydarren directors, Richard Foreman and Alderman William Thompson, lived in the house.

The rising climaxed on June 3 with a pitched battle between the soldiers and 10,000 rioters at the Castle Inn, half a mile from Penydarren House. One of the Highlanders, Donald Black, was stabbed in the hip. The rebels, armed with knives, scythes, pikes and the odd gun, retreated to a ridge above the Brecon Road near the village of Cefn Coed which became their headquarters. Penydarren House, perched on its plateau, gave their opponents a clear view of the insurgents, brandishing their weapons and waving a red flag which had been dipped in calf's blood. Lieutenant Colonel Richard Morgan of the Glamorgan Militia established his command there, with three-hundred soldiers bivouacked in and around the house. In the following days, Penydarren House only narrowly escaped a full-blown attack and although the rising effectively ended on June 6 when a crowd of rioters melted away before a group of heavily armed soldiers, the crisis dragged on for several more days. Richard Lewis,

Dic Penderyn, a young miner, was convicted of wounding the soldier Donald Black and was hanged in Cardiff in August, a working class martyr in a town named for martyrs.

Events of a cultural, if often no less confrontational, nature took over Penydarren Park in 1881 and 1901 when national eisteddfodau were held there. Music, at a time when the great Welsh choral competitions aroused a passion only rugby can match today, dominated these festivals. On both occasions the best-known musical adjudicator was one of Merthyr's great achievers, Joseph Parry, perhaps the greatest composer Wales has produced. The treatment meted out by the media to today's hapless rugby and soccer coaches appears a model of restraint compared to the insults heaped on the adjudicators of these competitions. They were routinely harassed and reviled, sometimes physically attacked. In 1881 it was Parry's turn. When he and a fellow judge withheld the prize for a cantata from a North Walian composer believed to be a shoe-in for the award, howls of protest at their flagrant 'prejudice' rose from the North Wales press. Parry felt particularly aggrieved since the assassination of his character resulted from a festival in his beloved home town.

Penydarren Park's life as a sporting stadium began in the 1880s when the Merthyr Athletic Club took it over as a venue for a variety of games and races. The pitch had a running track and a course for horse trotting races. In 1902 it was sub-let to the Merthyr Football Club, a founder-member of the Welsh Rugby Union. But when the club collapsed after many of its players defected to Merthyr's professional rugby league side, the way was open for Penydarren Park to become the home of Merthyr soccer. In 1908, it was taken over by

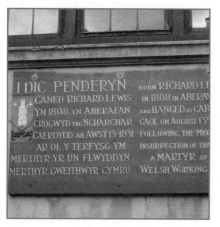

Merthyr Town AFC, a founder-member of the Third Division of the Football League in 1920. It routinely played Queens Park Rangers, Plymouth Argyle, Portsmouth, Reading, Newport County and Swansea. It met the likes of Arsenal and Wolverhampton Wanders in the FA Cup. A decade later, a series of disastrous results saw the side relegated from the Football League. It never returned.

Support plummeted and in 1934 it folded. The town would have to wait eleven years, and live through World War II, before a new club, Merthyr Tydfil, rose from the ashes. The new team would earn itself the label as the best outside the Football League. It never managed to join that league largely because at that time Penydarren Park hosted a second sport. For years it had been going to the dogs several times a week.

## PENYDARREN PARK – NIMROD

Every Thursday and Saturday evenings, for decades, the chatter of footballers on Penydarren Park gave way to the ear-piercing yelps of dogs chasing a mechanical hare around the lumpy grass track that bordered the pitch. But if greyhound racing gave some the masochistic pleasure of watching their money disappear into the pockets of bookmakers, for most it was a millstone around the neck of Merthyr's most famous institution in the years following World War II.

For a decade Merthyr Tydfil AFC, formed in 1945, dominated the Southern League, one step below the Football League. It won the championship four times in five years and came a close second in the fifth. Its right to a Football League place was undeniable. Yet each time it applied, it was rejected. The reason given was its greyhound track. The moralising elders of the Football League had ruled in 1946 that no team whose pitch pandered to the working class's addiction to gambling would be admitted. By the time the ruling had changed both the Penydarren Park track and Merthyr's reputation as the best side outside the League had long since disappeared. But if greyhound racing at Penydarren Park – despite the name a few hundred yards the Merthyr side of the border with Penydarren – was at best a mixed blessing, it could shed a side light on perhaps the most enigmatic figure of World War II.

During the war years when Merthyr was without a professional football side, greyhound racing continued at the park. Most Saturdays, a perky young soldier with a cheeky grin, a West Country accent as broad as the Cheddar Gorge and a tan the colour of teak, alighted from the Abergavenny train at the village of Cefn Coed on the outskirts of Merthyr. With him was a greyhound. His first call was to the Railway Inn in front of the station. He would sit in a corner, his dog at his feet, drinking pint after pint of beer and enjoying the 'crack' with the locals. As evening approached he would leave with the dog and trot the two miles to Penydarren Park where Nimrod, named after the mythical hunter and the founder of the Hun tribe, had been entered in a race.

The dog's owner, according to his soldier-trainer, was the most famous German prisoner taken during World War II. Rudolph Hess had the saturnine looks of a non-Aryan, a lantern jaw with a permanent six o'clock shadow and the haunted eyes of a man whose obsessions have passed into delusion and madness. Until a fateful day in 1941, he had been the second most powerful figure in Nazi Germany, Hitler's deputy and the man who would have taken over the running of the war should anything happen to the führer. Then at Augsburg on May 10, eighteen months into the war, the former World War I pilot climbed into the cockpit of a Me110 fighter plane and took off for a remote estate in Scotland that belonged to the Duke of Hamilton, whom Hess had known before the conflict. He crash-landed a few miles from his destination and was quickly arrested. Within days, Churchill had personally travelled to Scotland to question him. Hess's arrival not surprisingly triggered a media furore and a fever of speculation about the purpose of his journey which has continued to this day. Theories have abounded including one about a British intelligence plot to lure the deputy führer to Britain. The most convincing explanation remains the obvious one, that the deluded Nazi was on a personal mission to broker his own peace between Germany and the Britain he admired.

He was held in a series of comfortable prisons until, in June 1942, he was transferred to Maindiff Court, a baroque nineteenth century country house built by the ironmaster Crawshay Bailey, which was situated two miles outside Abergavenny. It had been used as an annex to the local mental hospital before Hess's arrival. There he spent the rest of the war before he was taken back to Germany to stand trial at Nuremberg for war crimes. He was convicted and locked up in Spandau Prison, Berlin, where he committed suicide, aged 93, in 1987.

During his years at Abergavenny, he spent much of the time walking the surrounding mountains accompanied by the greyhound, given to him as a companion, and a phalanx of guards which included the soldier, whose trips with Nimrod to the races at Penydarren Park became part of local folklore. Sadly, history tells us nothing of the dog's success at those Saturday night races, nor of his fate after his master had returned to Germany.

## PONTMORLAIS

Athens and Rome carefully preserve their ancient ruins, thousands of years old, as proof of their genius. Merthyr's fine buildings, often less than a hundred years old but disintegrating with neglect and decay, mock the town's claim to take its epoch-making past seriously. Pontmorlais, that part of Merthyr High Street leading to the town centre, is the product of the three decades that bridged the nineteenth and twentieth centuries when the town's leaders set out to forge a new civic identity and pride. It was the era when Merthyr, an expanding community of 80,000 pockmarked by extremes of wealth and poverty, by high levels of crime and disease, had long outgrown its puny public amenities. It lacked sanitation, a decent water supply, an adequate police force, hospitals, state schools, good roads. The building of the General Hospital in the 1880s and of the town hall a decade later marked this commitment to creating a town fit for its energetic, enterprising people. In 1905, it received its Royal Charter. It was now entitled to a motto, a seal and a coat of arms with the figure of St Tydfil, the fifth century Christian martyr on whose grave Merthyr's parish church is reputedly built and who gave her name to the town. Four years later it became a county borough.

That burgeoning sense of pride and achievement was reflected in the fine buildings and sense of space which epitomised Pontmorlais. At its southern threshold, on a ridge above Pontmorlais Circus, stood the tall, elegantly-proportioned YMCA, which, with its colonnaded redbrick and terracotta façade, was designed to nurture a commitment to the new civic values in the young. It housed a games room, a billiard room, a lecture hall, a café, a gym, even a rifle range!

Below it, a broad promenade extended north for almost a mile to the stolid, red-brick, unmistakeably late-Victorian General Hospital. For much of that journey the promenade, edged with sturdy iron railings, ran alongside Penydarren Park and the Georgian beauty of Penydarren House. Here, proud Merthyr could parade its Sunday best below the

canopy of the park's trees. On a
stepped and shrubbed terrace
above the promenade stood
more government and local
government buildings, their
terracotta facades echoing the
design of the YMCA a few
yards south. Between them on
its plinth of Portland Stone
stood the War Memorial
sculpted by the prolific L.S.
Merrifield and unveiled in
1931. Its centrepiece was the
bronze figure of St Tydfil, her

face hooded in a shawl, her head bowed as she wept for her lost
children.

Further north on the opposite side of the road stood the town's
cultural heart, the castellated walls of the imposing Theatre Royal,
opened in 1894 and equipped with fashionably new electric lighting,
an auditorium holding 1800 people, the latest machinery for moving
scenery and a massive stage measuring fifty feet by 30 feet which was
capable of holding a carriage and four horses. Three bars catered for
customers thirsting for a drink between long acts. Many of the most
famous theatrical and operatic names of the day appeared there
including the stars of the D'Oyly Carte, the Grand English Opera
Company and F.R. Benson's Shakespearian company.

Commercial Pontmorlais in the early years of the twentieth
century matched the confidence and optimism of its cultural and
civic life. There were top quality jewellers, tailors, tobacconists and
upmarket Italian cafés. The Palace Cinema boasted an opulently
marbled art deco façade. Fifty yards south, the graceful Tiger, later
Imperial, Hotel, hosted Merthyr's professional elite.

Pontmorlais played a major part in the life of the Basinis, as it did
in the lives of every other Merthyr family. At the beginning of World
War II my eldest sister was taken in by a generous-hearted
Pontmorlais Italian and his wife while she waited for her father to
return from internment as an enemy alien. In the late Fifties I was one
of the horde, quivering with excitement, which flowed irresistibly out
of Cyfarthfa Castle Grammar School and down the long drive to the
park gates, where a fleet of buses waited to take us to the Palace.
There we howled and screamed and wet ourselves as we celebrated a

turning point in western culture, the arrival of rock and roll in the films of Bill Haley and His Comets.

The buildings on Pontmorlais housed a series of important ministries and local government departments such as the social security offices, the Board of Trade, the Registrar, the borough's education offices. I called there to renew my passport for trips to Italy and as a student, I would arrive at the YMCA, housing the Education Department, to pick up my generous grant cheques from a local authority which preached equality of opportunity and put its money where its mouth was.

Now forty years on the damp, astringent stench of decay hangs perpetually on Pontmorlais. The shocking pink paint besmirching the Theatre Royal symbolises its humiliating tumble down the cultural ladder from theatre and opera house to cinema and finally to part-time bingo hall. Even that threadbare existence is over. It is now boarded up and decaying. Close by, the row of lively stores and cafés is gone, replaced by Chinese take-aways and second-hand shops bartering mounds of shabby goods. Only the iconic Flooks the Jewellers remains and that has been sold. A car park occupies the site of the Palace.

Across the road as I write, the YMCA crumbles into death, its brick-work and decoration decaying, its rich collection of windows – arched, bayed, rectangular – broken, boarded up and rotting. Part of the promenade below is blocked off and filthy. As once the government buildings further north echoed the YMCA's stunning design, now they repeat its slide towards terminal decline. Most tragic of all, vandals have ripped out the heart of Merrifield's beautiful War

Memorial. Its central alcove is empty, the weeping figure of St Tydfil torn down and damaged. South of Pontmorlais the catastrophe continues. The Miners Hall, once a chapel reputedly built by the great Victorian engineer, Isambard Kingdom Brunel, has been destroyed by two fires. Only a burned-out shell remains. Down Bethesda Street, the council-owned early nineteenth century Vulcan House, once

home to the foundry owner, Unitarian minister and fervent chartist, David John, faces probably its last chance of survival. The splendid Victorian town hall has also fallen into near-terminal decay.

A succession of local authority reports and schemes and private initiatives have been unveiled to save these and other remnants of Merthyr's fine architectural and historic heritage. Most never left the debating chamber. New schemes backed by passionate advocates, like Huw Lewis, the town's Welsh Assembly AM, might yet succeed. But as each plan fades into memory, time marches irresistibly to its conclusion, the point where decay demands demolition.

Unlike the Victorian melodramas which once enthralled audiences crammed into the Theatre Royal, this tragedy lacks a clear-cut villain. The burden carried by a small and impoverished local authority is illustrated by CADW's list of Merthyr's buildings and artefacts protected for their historic and architectural value. It contains more than two-hundred items. The authority is hamstrung by the fact that it does not own many of them. But critics highlight what they see as the council's indifference to the heritage of Wales's most important industrial town. Too many in the civic centre, the critics say, still regard its old buildings as expensive white elephants, blind to their potential for cultural and economic development. Perhaps the attitudes of previous councillors still lives – that Merthyr's heritage reminds us of cruel and exploitative ironmasters and the sooner it disappears the better.

Lost treasures, like the eighteenth century Old Iron Bridge across the River Taff, only the second to be built in Britain, dismantled in the Sixties and left to rot in a council yard, and The Triangle's collection of early nineteenth century workers' houses demolished in the Seventies, are indelible blots on the authority's record. Critics of the cash-strapped council point out that new sources of funding – from the lottery and the European Union – offer fresh hope of saving Merthyr's historic buildings, if only it has the will and expertise to exploit them. Meanwhile, twenty miles away along the Heads of the

Valleys Road, the little town of Blaenavon with an ironmaking history less important than Merthyr's, illustrates the economic benefits of heritage. Having won recognition as a World Heritage Site, its carefully-restored industrial remains, its museums, including the nearby Big Pit coal mine, and its visitor centre now attract almost 200,000 tourists a year. Industrial heritage, coupled with the inspirational

move of making Blaenavon a 'book town', promises a future for an old industrial community once dying on its feet. Its example shames its older and more illustrious neighbour.

## PONTMORLAIS – ZOAR CHAPEL

The five of us who sit around a table, in what was the vestry of one of Merthyr's oldest and most elegant chapels, are indulging in a pastime that was once as important a pillar of the town's identity as nonconformity. Now it is an activity as esoteric as chapel-going. We are talking Welsh. Our group of learners, including a teacher, a civil servant, a factory worker and the proprietor of a tea shop in the Brecon Beacons, is fairly advanced, concentrating on honing conversational skills. It is, like hundreds of others around Wales, the rump of a much larger beginners' class, what remains when the first flush of enthusiasm has been replaced by the prospect of years of hard grind. On the wall above us, a series of cartoons offers a thumbnail history of the chapel and of the Welsh language in Merthyr. But there is no hint of the time when the town played a key role in the nineteenth century explosion of Welsh literature and scholarship that forged a new sense of national identity and fuelled the demand for self-government.

For Wales's first industrial town, a magnet for immigration, a byword for cosmopolitan culture, was also perhaps the nation's most important centre for Welsh-language publishing and journalism. It became the cradle of one of the glories of nineteenth century Welsh

culture, choral singing. And it produced scholars who shaped the literary renaissance out of which grew great writers like the novelist Daniel Owen. Here the delights of Welsh medieval literature were revealed to a world-wide audience through Charlotte Guest's translation of the *Mabinogion* into English.

Even before the industrial revolution the agricultural community that flourished around the village of Merthyr Tydfil grew poets, philosophers and natural scientists: Hywel Rees, for example, an eighteenth century poet who farmed the slopes above Pontsarn, the beauty spot on the Taff Fechan River to where, two hundred years later, hundreds of us would decamp on bank holidays. His son Rhys, a stonemason, was also a poet, philosopher, and famous astronomer. Many of the poets and scholars produced by the industrial evolution were, like Lady Charlotte, immigrants, drawn to Merthyr by its spectacular growth and its abundant opportunities. Among the most important of them was Taliesin Williams, the son of the notorious Edward Williams, Iolo Morganwg, great poet, pioneering cultural historian and forger of poetry he claimed had been written many centuries before. Taliesin was himself a poet and scholar as well as his father's most devoted disciple. He spent much of his life lovingly preparing Iolo's chaotic manuscripts for publication. He had been born in 1787, probably at Cardiff where his father was in prison for debt. Brought up in the family home in the Vale of Glamorgan, he became a schoolteacher and worked for a time as an assistant at an academy in Neath. By 1816, Taliesin had set up his famous school in Merthyr where the sons and daughters of prominent industrialists, businessmen, doctors, lawyers and artists were educated.

Among Taliesin's friends was the chemist Thomas Stephens whose shop stood on Merthyr High Street opposite St David's Church. A handsome man with a beard and an undulating flow of hair, he stares out from a fading photograph poised between pride, self-possession and a wistful longing. He was born at Pontneddfechan in the Neath Valley. He came to Merthyr as an apprentice, eventually taking over the business. After long days selling his potions, he would spend his nights above the shop poring by candlelight over ancient texts and writing. His essays in both English and Welsh earned him an international reputation as one of the sharpest and most intelligent critics of the age. His eisteddfod essay in English on the literature of Wales from the twelfth century was published as *The Literature of the Kymry* and quickly recognised as a classic. He was unflinchingly rational and honest, sweeping away the obfuscations and cant of rivals.

His honesty inevitably earned him trouble. He wrote an essay for the 1858 Llangollen Eisteddfod on the subject of Madoc, the Welsh prince who allegedly discovered America before Columbus. The essay, concluding the story was a myth, was recognised as the best in the competition. But the judges denied him the prize on the grounds that it was not on the given subject. The competition required essays which supported the veracity of the Madoc story, they claimed. Disliking his stance, they changed the rules in order to rob him of the prize. The incident stained the reputation of the eisteddfod movement and drenched the organisers in the public's contempt. Stephens never wrote for an eisteddfod again. He played a prominent part in every aspect of Merthyr's public life, from education to health and politics. Controversy has continued to surround his reputation. He believed that English, with its world-wide influence, should be the language of a Welsh child's education and of public life in Wales. Welsh should be kept for poetry, for cultural competitions and the hearth. Those views have earned him the censure of modern critics like the novelist Emyr Humphreys.

The plethora of influential newspapers in Welsh and English produced in Merthyr included the radical Chartist publications, *Udgorn Cymru* (The Trumpet of Wales) and *The Advocate and Merthyr Free Press*. Among the most influential Welsh language newspapers, which was printed in Merthyr but distributed throughout Wales, was *Y Tyst a'r Dydd*, (The Witness and the Day), later *Y Tyst*. The paper was linked with the Welsh Independent nonconformist denomination and its editor for many years was the Rev John Thomas, pastor of Zoar Chapel. It still survives.

Zoar has joined the long list of Merthyr chapels which have closed because they can no longer command a congregation. But its role in the town's public life continues. There are plans to convert it into a community arts centre. Meanwhile, its vestry has become a centre for Welsh language learning in a town where the number of Welsh speakers plummeted for most of the twentieth century. Now it is rising.

Almost 6,000 can speak Welsh in the borough, around eleven per cent of the total population, a figure which has grown by around four per cent in the past decade. There are two Welsh language primary schools, one of which is among the biggest in Wales. But there is still no secondary school and six-hundred Merthyr children have to travel to Aberdare in the next valley for their Welsh medium education.

If there is little knowledge of Merthyr's rich past as a centre for Welsh culture among today's Welsh speakers, perhaps that is no bad thing. Unburdened by an awareness of that past, those now learning the language retain the fiery commitment of pioneers trekking through hostile territory. Their leader is the dark, intense but patient James Bevan, born less than two miles from Zoar in the steepling streets of Twynyrodyn. The product of parents who are themselves learners, Jamie went to school in Rhydyfelin, lower down the Taff Valley. He encourages his charges with stories of strangers met in bank queues or in supermarkets who turn out to be Welsh speakers. It is as if they form part of a shadowy resistance movement who recognise each other through nods and smiles and brief greetings.

The enemy is everywhere. After class in the vestry we cross the road to Yr Angor, the Anchor, one of Merthyr's oldest and most welcoming pubs. We join other Welsh speakers clustered in the bar. Our numbers include a personal friend Roger Howell, a retired teacher home after a career spent in England, builders, factory workers, class-room assistants, strong-armed, strong willed women. Their commitment is epitomised by Roger who, starting to learn the language in his sixties, has achieved fluency.

The Welsh is loud and often inaccurate, the chatter underscored by tension. Clustered at the opposite end of the bar – a matter of feet in the narrow, claustrophobic Anchor – sit a group of sullen English workers. There is puzzlement in their faces, and resentment at what they regard as the perversity of those who speak perfectly good English but who insist on using this guttural 'foreign' language. It is a reaction Welsh speakers are used to. And the hurt caused by strangers is nothing compared to the pain generated by your own. Jamie Bevan recalls talking Welsh with a friend in a local restaurant when a man at the next table turned and leaned over to him, his face livid with anger.

"Why don't you speak English? I can't understand a word of that fucking language." The accent, like the man, was unmistakeably Merthyr.

## TRAMROADSIDE

Turn left off the High Street at Pontmorlais, past the monument to Richard Trevithick which flanks the Theatre Royal, past the rear entrance to the Penydarren End, the pub, now a corner shop, where you forged lifelong friendships, across what was once the bridge spanning the Morlais Brook and you come to a narrow lane bordered on one side by a rubbish-strewn embankment and on the other by a cottage and the shabby, cat-infested backyards of stores and flats. A walk at night along its dimly-lit length raises a frisson of fear. It is the perfect place for a mugging.

This is yet another dusty corner of Merthyr whose scruffy present masks its historic past. Along this lane, two hundred years ago, trundled and snorted Richard Trevithick's Penydarren engine on its way from the ironworks to the Glamorgan Canal at Abercynon. It was the first steam-driven railway journey in the world, heralding a new era. And if that journey proved to be a false dawn – it would be decades before the problems thrown up by steam railways could be fully solved – horse-drawn trams continued to carry the products of the Penydarren and the Dowlais Works down the tracks to the canal and on to Cardiff. Even when the arrival of the Taff Vale Railway robbed the tramroad of its traffic, trains from nearby collieries still used the rails to carry household coal and miners to and from work. The tramroad was a parallel universe to that of the High Street a few feet away. It was a rival commercial centre, lined with shop fronts. A chapel and terraces of houses opened on to it. Then, like now, women walking alone at night were happy to give it a wide berth. It comes most vividly to life in the pages of its most famous inhabitant, a writer born one hundred and twenty years ago who still makes a strong claim to being the best Merthyr has yet produced.

Not surprisingly given his poverty-stricken upbringing and his lack of education – by the age of twelve he had begun work with his father down a Merthyr mine – Jack Jones was a late starter as a writer. He did not publish his first novel until he was fifty. Making up for lost time, he spent the next three decades of his long life pouring millions of words into eleven novels, three volumes of autobiography, a biography of his friend David Lloyd George, plays and hundreds of radio scripts. Many, but not enough, of the thousands of pages he filled ended up in his editor's waste basket. Many of those which escaped into print are marred by hyperbole, crude characterisation, long passages of undigested history, tedious authorial interventions and narrative tricks which all too quickly become stylistic ticks and mannerisms. He died less than forty years ago, but the contemporary taste for minimalist prose and fabulist plots has banished his works to an occasional second-hand bookseller on the Internet and the stacks of local libraries.

At his best in a handful of novels such as the Merthyr trilogy, *Bidden to the Feast*, *Black Parade* and *Off to Philadelphia in the Morning*, the fictionalised story of Joseph Parry, and in the first volume of autobiography, *Unfinished Journey*, the writing is fresh and vibrant. No-one is better at conjuring up the noise, the stench, the vigour, the colour and the cruelty of his native town, still riding a wave of prosperity in the decades before the Great Depression.

Much of the attraction of *Unfinished Journey* lies in the astonishing story it has to tell. The boy who left elementary school at twelve to join his father down a Merthyr mine went on to become a professional soldier, addicted gambler, miners' agent, politician and one of the best-known public speakers in Britain, before settling into the life of a writer, a life won through sheer hard work, persistence and force of will. Trying to follow the hairpin bends of his political career is enough to give the reader vertigo. He began, predictably, as a communist. A meeting with Lloyd George turned him into a parliamentary candidate for the Liberal Party. Later, attracted to Oswald Moseley's New Party, he travelled Britain speaking on its behalf, although he vehemently denied he was ever a fascist. Later still, he briefly supported the Conservatives and then hastened to back that curious cross between a religious faith and a political party, Moral Re-armament. But nobody could accuse him of trimming his sails to suit his own selfish interests. Each twist in his complex life was made with the passion of a true convert. He poured all of himself into everything he pursued. More often than not, his choices landed him and his family in deep financial trouble. When he started gambling it consumed him, leaving him, his wife and new child homeless. When he finally took up writing it was with a commitment that brought him

and his loved ones once more to the brink of financial ruin.

He was born in a terrace of a hovels called Tai Harri Blawd at the northern end of the Tramroad, behind the Penydarren End and a few yards from his beloved Theatre Royal. The cramped cottages were topped by an even meaner row of single story dwellings. They formed a double-decker slum. In front of the houses, the Morlais Brook flowed between the two bridges which gave Pontmorlais its name. Two filthy earth privies flanked each row, totally inadequate to the needs of the large families crammed into them. (His beloved mother Saran, short for Sarah Ann, bore fifteen chidlren, nine of whom survived into adulthood.) So the children – and adults who were caught short – defecated on the left bank of the brook which hummed with ordure. The banks of the brook were infested by rats as large as cats. The Morlais's sobriquet 'Stinky', which we used as children, was well-earned. Now, culverted and only briefly visible as it passes through Pontmorlais, the brook is once more a clear, sweet-smelling mountain stream, an ironic comment on Merthyr's current economic difficulties.

A telling episode from *Unfinished Journey* rams home the quality of life in Tai Harri Blawd, long since demolished. Jack, aged six or seven, is run over by the drunken driver of a coal cart. The child is bed-ridden while the leg in its plaster sheath mends. From the start it itches unbearably, a side effect of the healing process the modern reader assumes. But the irritation drives the child into near-delirium. When the doctor arrives to cut the plaster off the true cause of his discomfort is revealed. Shuddering with distaste, Dr Ward sees the plaster is alive with bed bugs.

Eventually the family escapes to a house in Penyard on the top of the hill above Tai Harri Blawd and the miasmic Morlais. Here the air is more salubrious, the house a little bigger with fewer vermin. But Jack's true escape, as it is for his mother, is into the world of magic conjured up by the circuses and the tented theatres which pitched next to the high street or on the nearby site of the demolished Penydarren Ironworks. Their excitement reaches fever pitch when the brand new Theatre Royal, with its daily fare of drama, melodrama and opera, opens just around the corner in 1894. Jack finds himself a night-time job selling sweets, biscuits and oranges to the audience. Occasionally, he and his friends are allowed on stage as extras in an extravagant Victorian epic.

In that theatre the child-miner learned to dream of a life beyond the pit, the pub and the chapel. The ambition seeded there would lead him to a creative life which, if it didn't result in untold riches and a villa in the South of France, at least made him a reputation as one of the best of the working class writers to emerge from the depressed Thirties. It bought him a comfortable life in a middle-class suburb of Cardiff his parents would never have dared dream of.

## MERTHYR IN CARDIFF

He haunted the upstairs bar of the Albert, the public house at the southern end of Cardiff's St Mary Street which was the watering hole of journalists like me who worked in the offices of the *Western Mail* and the *South Wales Echo* a few yards away. When he knew who I was and where I had come from he buttonholed me with the insistence of Coleridge's Ancient Mariner. And if his story did not have the same hypnotic fascination, it was more interesting than most. In his mid seventies, with a mass of greasy, grey-white hair and thick horn-rimmed glasses, his fingers stained a deep brown by the untipped cigarettes he chain-smoked, he had the patrician looks of actor Patrick Cargill, star of the Seventies sitcom *Father Dear Father*. He had himself struggled, with little success, to become an actor, a fact betrayed by the careful exaggeration of the received English he spoke through constantly puckered lips and his precise, theatrical gestures. He was, despite the accent, the son, grandson and great-grandson of miners some of whom had spent sixty years working twelve-hour shifts in the bellies of decrepit, dangerous Valley pits. They and their many children lived in vermin-infested houses their despairing, house-proud wives struggled hopelessly to keep clean.

His name was Clifford Jones and we often talked deep into the afternoon. He lived in the heart of the city's bed-sit land, Cathedral Road. I would eventually write about a life that had included a six-year spell in Egypt as professional soldier, his wounding in France in 1940 and his attempts after World War II to become a film actor. But our conversations most often revolved around the one relationship that had dominated his life – with the powerful, indomitable, intim-idating father who by sheer will had overcome massive handicaps to succeed in everything Cliff had struggled to do and had failed. He was the second son of Merthyr-born Jack Jones, the self-taught polymath and linguist who had been miner, soldier, politician, speech-maker, international traveller, playwright, novelist and broadcaster.

Cliff's attitude to Jack, who had died in 1970, almost twenty years before his son and I met, oscillated between a childlike hero worship and angry resentment. Jack, whom I had never met, was clearly a compelling physical presence despite his diminutive stature – he was a slight 5ft 5ins. Cliff accused his father of being a tyrant with a hair-trigger temper who submitted his family to his iron will. His thirst for achievement meant that the late-developing writer invariably put the demands of his career before the needs of his large family. Cliff complained that the novelist, racked by the loss of his two youngest sons – the brilliant Oxford graduate, Lawrence, who died of his wounds after winning the Military Cross in the Middle East in 1942, and David who died of tuberculosis soon after the end of World War II, treated him with dismissive contempt. The son attributed much of his failure to fulfil his artistic potential to his father's hostility.

Cliff's portrait had, superficially at least, its persuasive points. If it is true that the novelist sometimes treated his family badly, he would merely have been repeating the pattern of his own father as portrayed in the autobiography *Unfinished Journey*. Dai Jones shared at least some of the character traits of the brutish miner Rhys Davies in his son's novel, *Bidden to the Feast*. Jack was acutely aware that his own behaviour in the early days of his marriage to the patient Laura was so negligent it made him a pariah shunned by, among others, his own mother. After his gambling addiction had forced his wife and child into near-destitution, he had to fight redeem himself in Laura's eyes with hard work in a succession of low-paid, menial jobs.

Perhaps it was guilt that made him react with so little sympathy when he saw Cliff neglect his own wife and three children to pursue a dream to become an actor in London. In his last volume of autobiography, *Give Me Back My Heart*, Jack Jones describes the moment when Cliff, the son he regards as the family's black sheep, pleads for the chance to continue acting. Jack's response is to tell the war veteran, injured before Dunkirk, to get a job in a Valleys mine. But the father is quick to acknowledge that the son's neglect of his family pales beside his own in the early years of his marriage. Jack's friend and fellow Merthyr writer, Glyn Jones, paints a tender portrait of his love for Laura in Glyn's book on Anglo-Welsh writers, *The Dragon Has Two Tongues*. The two writers and their wives would meet in the Cardiff house of a third, Gwyn Jones. By then Laura had become very deaf. Jack would take care not to leave her out of the conversation, painstakingly explaining what had just been said.

Jack Jones's appetite for work was voracious enough to invoke a shaming sense of inadequacy even in the conscientious Glyn Jones. Plagued by constant money worries, harried by the tumult of a young and noisy family, Jack, a miner at twelve with virtually no formal education, struggled against a tide of indifference and a flood of rejections to produce millions of words and, eventually, an important literary reputation. It was inevitable that such a journey would produce family casualties. The value of Clifford Jones's portrait of his father lies in the insight it gives into the price his career exacted from the man who became one of Merthyr's best-known chroniclers.

# WEST

## SWANSEA ROAD, JOHNNY OWEN

I might have served him – with a threepenny cornet, perhaps, or a sixpenny wafer, or a packet of fruit pastilles, the huge brown eyes staring up at me from beneath the slick of black hair, the right fist that would take him to the brink of a world title and bring death instead outstretched to offer me a few grubby coppers. I would have been in my last year at grammar school preparing for university. He would have been five years old, the long skeletal face winged by elephant ears already wearing the enigmatic smile that expressed an awkward shyness, a moment's apprehension, a bottomless courage. The Gellideg council estate, Swansea Road, to anybody born within twenty miles of it, into which Johnny Owen had been born was on the daily route of the Basini family's purpose-built ice-cream and sweets van, tall and ugly by today's sleek standards and without those charmless insistent chimes that send parents into a fury. We slid open a window and bellowed our presence.

My brother and I, in different grammar schools, would divide Saturdays and sometimes Sundays between us to give my father a rest. On Saturdays, the Swansea Road estate was the last call on the morning shift, the one you did if your school rugby side was not playing or had a home fixture. The estate, built after World War II, was a bleak place, row after row of identikit council houses, each with a concrete, flat-roofed porch, each fronted by a fenceless, featureless expanse of grass studded by shallow steps. The streets toppled down the bare western slopes of the Aberdare Mountain defenceless against the year-round driving rain and the winter blizzards. The breathtaking panorama across the valley to the ordered acres of Cyfarthfa Park, topped by the wild beauty of the ruined Morlais Castle and fronted by the elegant curve of Cefn railway viaduct, did little to reconcile the residents to their drab fate.

It was not an obvious place in which to nurture heroism, but Johnny Owen was an authentic hero who, frail to the point of ridicule, saw the terrible dangers in his chosen profession of boxing and faced them unflinchingly. Dedicated, respectful, conscientious, he recognised early that his talent would make him the chief provider for his big family, seven brothers and sisters as well as his mother and father. He accepted the role with alacrity. His father Dick, a miner and factory worker turned boxing trainer and, finally, keeper of his son's flame, introduced him to boxing early, refereeing the matches between Johnny and his elder sister in the cramped front room of their house in Heol Bryn Padell. Dick transmitted his passion for the sport to all five of his sons. But it was Johnny who found in boxing the challenge that would focus his life. This pathologically shy, awkward, freakishly thin boy had found his means of self-expression and, like a great writer or painter, he would hone his new skills obsessively, in his case to the point where they would kill him. His ferocious ambition made him train with a dedication that would leave his friends and fellow boxers shaking their heads in disbelief as they walked away. He would run, time and again, backwards up Sanatorium Hill, a giddyingly steep road leading up from Pontsarn in the countryside north of Merthyr. He spent hour after hour chopping down trees until the alarmed landowner told him he was denuding his property. He made a virtue of the stick-thin torso and the ribcage that pressed through his skin like the gnarled roots of the trees he cut down. As a professional, he eagerly adopted the nickname The Matchstick Man. He would walk into the ring behind a banner featuring a skeleton. He had a long apprenticeship as an amateur, fighting 124 times and losing just eighteen.

His rise to the top as a professional was rapid. In four years he won the British and European titles, losing just one of his twenty-seven fights. By Autumn 1980, the crowning moment of his career beckoned. On September 19 at the bear pit Olympic Auditorium in a Latin suburb of Los Angeles he fought the Mexican Lupe Pintor for the World Bantamweight Championship. The odds were stacked against him. Pintor had been hardened by an upbringing of extreme poverty presided over by a violent, single-parent father into a street fighter who refused to acknowledge defeat. He was skilful, experienced and he punched harder than the Welshman. The auditorium was packed with howling Mexicans who showered Owen's few hardy fans with emptied beer cans filled with their urine. Johnny's purse was just £13,000, less than his hero Jimmy Wilde, 'the ghost with the hammer', received for fighting for a world title fifty-seven years earlier. But Owen knew that if he won it would be the start of better pay nights and of the fulfilment of his most pressing ambition, to make his family financially comfortable.

For the first half of the fifteen-round fight Johnny looked as if he was about to clinch that ambition. He outboxed the Mexican, constantly punishing him with his powerful and accurate right jab. Then in the ninth round Pintor finally caught him. The frail-looking Welshman had been knocked down for the first time in his career. He rose to his feet too quickly for those in his corner, his father Dick and manager Dai Gardiner, who wanted him to take a few seconds more to recover. Even then it looked as if he might snatch a remarkable victory as he pounded away at the Mexican's bloodied face. Until the twelfth when Pintor's vicious uppercut sent him to the canvas once more. This time there would be no recovery. As he lay there, the horrific truth dawned on his father and manager. That brutal punch had sent Johnny into a coma. Hospital examinations would reveal that his exceptionally strong jaw refused to break under the impact of Pintor's blow. Instead the Mexican's fist drove the jaw bone up through the Welshman's abnormally thin skull and into his brain. The damage was irreparable. He lay unconscious in the nearby California Hospital for seven weeks before he died on November 4 1980, aged twenty-four. His stricken parents began the long journey home with his coffin.

Ten thousand people, a sixth of Merthyr's population turned out for his funeral on a bleak, wet Armistice Day. The 160 car procession stretched the length of the town from the High Street Baptist Chapel in the south to Pant Cemetery in the north. I covered the funeral for the *Western Mail*. Scores of stars from sport, entertainment and journalism huddled in their black-windowed limousines, but the chief mourner alongside the Owen family was the town itself, grieving the passing of a son who summed up so much of what was best in it.

Johnny could not have been more different from many of the boys he grew up with on Swansea Road, quiet, generous and respectful where they were – are – loud arrogant, violent, bent on destruction. Where they, still in their teens, fought to assert their manhood by impregnating girls even younger than they were, Johnny concentrated on his profession, preferring, he said, to leave courtship and marriage to the days after the ring. It was a sensible and admirably self-disci-plined attitude, given the dangers he faced; but one so old-fashioned it prompted, even in journalists who admired him, the gently-mocking tag of 'the virgin solider'. Where his contemporaries aped pop stars and local hard-men, he hero-worshipped yet another great local champion, Jimmy Wilde as frail as he was, who had been born in the south of the Merthyr borough, at Quaker's Yard, although he did not learn to box until he had moved to the Rhondda when he was twelve.

Johnny Owen movingly recorded his values in the diary he kept. Before fighting John Feeney for the British Bantamweight title in June 1980, his last before the bout with Pintor, he wrote: "Must put everything into training and go to bed early so I can win and start earning money for a pub or a hotel. A good win on national TV will do you a power of good and, if you can stay unbeaten through 1980, you will have achieved all that you wanted".

The words echo with tragic irony.

# SOUTH

## BETHESDA STREET – GARTHNEWYDD

With its cream walls, overhanging roofs edged in deep, dull pink and porch hoods shaped like upturned snow shovels, its architectural style is best descried as ski chalet chic. The block of housing association flats curves around the junction of two of Merthyr's most historic streets: Brecon Road along which the insurgents of the 1831 rising marched behind their white flag dipped red in calf's blood, and Bethesda Street at the bottom of which once stood Joseph Parry's Bethesda Chapel and the start of China, Merthyr's notorious red light district. Opposite stands the late Victorian St Mary's Roman Catholic Church. A few doors down in Bethesda Street is the building once known as 'The Rooms', large and barrack-like, which housed organisations spun-off by St Mary's, such as the Catholic Young Men's Society. Later it became a pub and restaurant, then a Chinese takeaway. Both are closed. A ground floor window is stuffed with an old divan bed. Steps lead from the street to what was once a pub garden now littered with the reliquaries of long-dead nights out; upturned tables and benches, a tall, broken, one-armed bandit.

Next to the flats, the Park View pub, where once my rugby master, the amiable Dan Jones, spent long hours each night plotting the success of his boys, has been refurbished and re-opened. Despite the pub's welcome, the corner's air of decay persists. The block of flats, Garthnewydd Court, was opened twenty-five years ago by the town's then MP, Ted Rowlands, an event marked by a plaque outside its electronically locked gate. It is already care-worn, the wood framing doors and windows sometimes splintered and in desperate need of paint brighter than its dull, dead pink. The bottom half of a steel-reinforced front door has been replaced by plasterboard. Some flats are empty, their entrance halls littered with unopened mail.

The corner's history illustrates one of Merthyr's enduring lessons, that crumbling houses and decaying streets often cradle the creative in the human spirit. On the spot now occupied by

Garthnewydd Court stood a large and imposingly ugly, three storied Victorian house with fourteen rooms in all. It had an arched wrought iron gate, a front garden and a gabled porch spacious enough to form an extra room. Its name, Garthnewydd, lives on in its successor. Once it had housed members of Merthyr's ruling elite: doctors and local politicians. Later one of the town's most successful entrepreneurs lived there, Henry Seymour Berry, estate agent, property developer and millionaire businessman. He left Garthnewydd in 1919, when he bought the vast Buckland Estate at Bwlch in the Breconshire countryside, ten miles north west of Merthyr. There he became Lord Buckland, and when he died in a tragic riding accident on his estate the Berry family gave Garthnewydd to Merthyr. Its civic functions included acting as a centre for the distribution of food and clothing during the worst of the Depression and as a headquarters for voluntary organisations. By the late 'fifties one of the house's trustees, a Quaker community worker named John Dennithorne, had invited a community of fellow pacifists, dedicated to living Gandhi's social philosophy, to set up house there. They were to leave their mark on the peace movement. Their library at Garthnewydd became the cornerstone of a collection now housed at the University of Bradford, famed for its Department of Peace Studies.

The pacifists were eager to open Garthnewydd's doors to those they considered fellow travellers, like Plaid Cymru. Which is how a garrulous, barrel-bellied, spade-bearded journalist, political activist and librarian arrived there in 1960. Harri Webb, born in Swansea and educated at Oxford University, had become the branch librarian at Dowlais, despite his lack of professional qualification. Soon the pacifist community had imploded under the pressure of their internecine quarrels. They moved out. By now the town had apparently lost track of who owned the decaying pile and Harri invited friends and fellow Welsh nationalists in to share his rent-free accommodation. Among those who joined him there were the teacher and Welsh language protest leader, Neil Jenkins, later Neil ap Siencyn and Pete Meazey, tall, engaging, with an endlessly welcoming grin. Pete, with a passion for folk music, would go on to open a book and record shop in Cardiff, indispensable to those interested in Wales. Eventually he would leave for Brittany.

The first to move in with Harri was a newly-qualified French teacher, Meic Stephens. He would become a journalist, Literature Director of the Welsh Arts Council, poet, influential editor, scholar, critic and university professor. Meic, tall fair-haired and angular, shared much with the smaller, darker, rounder Harri. Both from Anglicised families, they had acquired an impressive command of Welsh. Both were committed left-wing nationalists who shared a passion for poetry. At Garthnewydd Meic would found a literary publisher, the Triskel Press, out of which grew one of Wales's longest-lived and most important literary periodicals, *Poetry Wales*. He played a key role in encouraging Harri Webb to begin publishing the poetry which, with its technical brilliance and its wide variety of style and content, would make him famous. Under their influence Garthnewydd would become a powerhouse in the literary and political life of Wales. Meic Stephens has written about those early years in the magazine, *Planet*. A variety of key figures such as the politicians Gwynfor Evans, Emrys Roberts and Phil Williams and the poets and editors Keidrych Rhys and Tony Conran stayed at the house. Harri Webb did not share the pacifist principles of the previous occupiers. He became increasingly convinced of the need for violence to free Wales. In a 1963 letter to Gwilym Prys Davies, Harri emphasised his commitment to Padraig Pearse's belief in the necessity of a 'blood-sacrifice' to win freedom for a nation. The founding father of the Irish republic felt it was necessary for a nation's leaders to shed blood in order to expiate the guilt of past generations who had failed to end its servitude. According to Meic Stephens, Harri designed the symbol, based on the White Eagle of Eryri (Snowdonia), which became the badge of the Free Wales Army.

It is not surprising, given their militancy, that members of the Garthnewydd nationalist community were in the thick of the direct action protests over the neglect of the Welsh language and its need for official status, organised by Cymdeithas yr Iaith Gymraeg, the Welsh Language Society. Meic Stephens was prominent in the first of those non-violent protests on Trefechan Bridge in Aberystwyth in January 1963.

I was a student at Aberystwyth at the time. As an Italian from Anglicised Merthyr I remember watching the protest with the baffled fascination of a traveller who has just arrived in an unknown country. It would take me years to make the chilling connection between the struggle of that ancient Welsh culture against the spectre of its death with the peasant culture of the North Italian Apennines, rich in language, poetry and humanity, into which my parents had been born and which I had grown to love. Its death rattle had already sounded.

## DOWLAIS LIBRARY

Of the half dozen buildings that remain to recall the dynamic Dowlais which was a world centre for the production of iron and steel, the town's library is the most flamboyant. A flourish in flame-red local sandstone of pilastered facades, cupola-gabled walls and scores of small square windows topped occasionally by large round ones, it once dominated a warren of mean terraces. Now it is isolated, except for the crumbling hulk of St John's Church standing opposite. The decay of the church, the burial place of Sir Josiah John Guest, merely emphasises the library's vigour. It was built one hundred years ago on land donated by the steelworks which spread for miles along the valley floor below. In its ponderous ostentation bordering on the vulgar, its self-consciously eclectic display of scholarship and technique, its constant demand for attention, not to mention its sense of the comic, the library reflects at least some of the qualities of the man who ran it for a decade in the 'fifties and the 'sixties.

Harri Webb, the people's bard with an untoppable talent for savage mockery of the prim, the pompous and the hypocritical – the Welsh establishment, in other words – could be an inspirational librarian with his wide-ranging erudition and his passion for Wales and its culture. But he was not, predictably, without his eccentricities. A dedicated campaigner for the Welsh he had learned as an adult, he would admonish those who dared to borrow a book about Wales in English by scribbling in the fly-leaf , "Cymraeg you bastards!" Perhaps preoccupied with a poem or his latest piece of polemical journalism, he was sometimes unwilling to go through the time-consuming business of replacing returned books on their shelves.

He would thrust them into the arms of the next hapless borrower urging, "Four books you want? Take these."

Achievements fizzed off him like fireworks. He was a hard-hitting journalist, a 'people's poet' dedicated to praising the 'gwerin' and lacerating their enemies, a love poet displaying deep feeling and a dazzling technique, an accomplished performer of his own work, a television scriptwriter and playwright. And he once stood as an MP. Perhaps his best-loved work is a song, the Welsh language poem 'Colli Iaith', Losing a Language, which, set to music by Meredydd Evans and sung by Heather Jones, could move a stone effigy to tears. It became an anthem of Welsh language activists in the 'sixties and 'seventies.

In English, he is remembered best for his lampoons, like 'Synopsis of The Great Welsh Novel', in which he pillories the sentimental melodramas of writers like Richard *How Green Was My Valley* Llewellyn, or Merthyr's own Jack Jones, and 'Our Budgie' in which his affectionate description of the petulant, self-serving, preening household pet, endlessly amused by its own antics, ends with the sledgehammer couplet,

> This futile bird, it seems to me,
> Would make a perfect Welsh MP.

Exasperated admirers as well as critics, frustrated by the dizzying variety of his work, complain of its lack of focus. He is a street entertainer, the bard of the bar-room and the television studio, too busy pandering to his public to be a 'proper poet'. He seemed eager to agree, denigrating his work in a poem like 'Waldo', a tribute to the Welsh language poet, Waldo Williams, his hero. But his love poetry like the 'Sonnets For Mali' or 'Henrhyd', written not merely in the fiendishly difficult sestina, a form appropriately developed by his spiritual ancestors, the troubadours, but a double sestina approaching the complexity of Welsh poetry's cynghanedd, displays his emotional power as well as his mastery of technique beyond most 'serious poets'. As Brian Morris, in his perceptive study of Harri Webb in the *Writers of Wales* series, points out his true subject, that which gave a unity to work as journalist, politician, poet and librarian, is his love for homeland.

> Sing for Wales or shut your trap –
> All the rest's a load of crap

was his advice to a young poet. It applies as much to politicians, teachers and roadsweepers. It is perhaps that subordination of everything to the collective cause which so galls those brought up in the English Liberal tradition, which views individual achievement as paramount. Sometimes his sense of mission leads him into mistakes which weaken his work's effectiveness as propaganda as well as its literary quality. The satire becomes too facile, his targets too obvious, as in 'The Old Leader'.

Harri, as befits a writer with the self-imposed duty of wooing the Welsh back to a love of their bloodied, enslaved but still beautiful country, was a very public poet and a gregarious man. He turned his rollicking nights with an army of friends and fellow travellers into rollicking verse. Most of those nights were spent in the legendary Lamb in Merthyr's Castle Street, black and white outside, dark brown and nicotine yellow inside, better known for it is raucous songs and loud argument than for its comfort. Harri's friend and literary executor, Meic Stephens, tellingly labels the pub's noisier and more aggressive customers, 'pint-pot patriots'. Harri himself blew away the fantasy-fuelled hot air given off by his louder comrades with a blast of gentle satire.

For all his sociability he remained a solitary man, evidenced by the loneliness that haunted his eyes. For whatever reason, he found it easier to love a landscape, a culture, a language than he did the individuals who forged them. The most unpromising of places could evoke in him a passion his lovers must have envied. Yet another Merthyr immigrant – he had been born in Swansea – he found a spiritual home in dirty, damp, depressing Dowlais and its loud library.

> That lift of wonder in the Lusiads
> When all the marvels of the eastern sea
> Sparkled and shone in endless mystery
> To daze the hungry eyes of Vasco's lads
> With scenes undreamt of, isles of luxury,
> Promises of pleasure, loot and mastery,
> Empire unheard of, opulent dowry,
> Indies on Indies dazzling myriads,
> Was mine when on an iron January day
> I first saw Dowlais on its iron hill
> And all was iron, like its history,
> The stone, the scowling church, the air
> All gave me welcome and all said
> At last, after long wandering, you're there.

## BETHESDA STREET – THE TANYARD

The stench permeates your memory; the aroma of cloying, honey-sweet cider, strong enough to rot the casks in which it was served, percolated through the stink of unwashed skin and clothes stiff with dirt. It brought your stomach gagging into your mouth. The black and white Tanyard Inn stood at the bottom of Bethesda Street close to the tanning yard that gave it its name. It had once been the northern border of the area labelled 'China, the Celestial Empire', mocking the thieves, the 'the nymphs of the pave' – the prostitutes – and their 'bullies', their pimps or protectors, who poured into it during the first half of the nineteenth century. With them came pickpockets, thieves, receivers, conmen, forgers, muggers, street fighters, ballad singers, entertainers and fairground performers drawn from all over the world by the prospect of easy money, the pleasures of the flesh and a life more or less free from interference by the law. For decades policemen refused to patrol there unless they were in twos or threes. And China had its 'emperors', men like John Jones, 'Shoni Sgubor Fawr', bare-knuckle mountain fighter, thief and pimp, who when things got too hot for him in Merthyr moved west with his friend 'Dai'r Cantwr', poet and ballad singer, to lead the Rebecca Riots. Both were arrested, tried and deported to Australia. If China was a dangerous 'no-go' area, where in an hour the unwary could lose a year's wage or even their lives, it was also a place of excitement and change where different languages and traditions melded to create fresh cultures, where the anarchic folk customs of rural Wales clashed with the more regimented social structures imposed by the new industrial society.

By the time I visited the Tanyard in the late Sixties, the hovels of China, lining the left bank of the River Taff had long since disappeared. Only lower Bethesda Street and a row or two of houses to the north remained to hint at what its 'Beggars Opera' society had been like. Many from those streets drank in the Tanyard. Like their predecessors they lived from hand to mouth – horse-trading, dealing in rags and scrap, a little stealing and receiving. If most of Chinas' raw satanic energy had long since leached out of their lives, some of its colour remained in their language and coarse, irreverent humour. As the town's dispossessed they were free from the preoccupations of jobs and families and homes. They helped to add the strain of unruly anarchy fundamental to Merthyr's character.

Their poet is Alan Osborne, teacher, artist, opera librettist and dramatist. In plays like *In Sunshine and in Shadow, Bull, Rock and Nut* and *The Redemption Song*, he captures the flamboyance of their language – a fusion of Welsh, South Wales English and Hollywood – their humour, violence, aimless despair. It was a vulnerable time for me when we drank together in the Tanyard. I had retreated home, haunted by family ghosts, by a relationship that refused to go smoothly, by the pressures of a demanding job. He unveiled his world to me shyly, hoping perhaps it would nourish my imagination as it had his. He would be disappointed. More likely, he wanted to show me the resilience, the will to survive, of those in my hometown who were far worse off than me. Whatever the reason, it worked. With his help and that of other friends, I was soon back to the challenges of daily journalism.

When the police and the magistrates finally tamed China in the second half of the nineteenth century many of the thieves, the 'nymphs' and their 'bullies' moved half a mile south to Ynysgau, lapping the steps of one of the town's biggest and oldest chapels. The district, populated by the boatmen who worked on the neighbouring Glamorgan Canal, was known locally as 'Under the Arch' because a narrow archway at its northern end was the only way into it from the town centre. It succeeded China as the target of denunciations from innumerable pulpits. When it was eventually flattened, its inhabitants were clustered in a featureless housing estate on a remote hillside on the outskirts of the town. Galon Uchaf was less than two miles away from my parents' café in Penydarren. We got used to the disreputable who had come 'from under the arch' calling in for sweets or cigarettes or a cup of tea. Among them was 'Lily the Dap', loud, dirty and obnoxious, with her crippled foot perpetually encased in the same filthy gym shoe. Lily's sole response to the world was ceaseless complaint, bellowed in a voice as raucous as a factory hooter. Her whine and the smell that went with it would drive me, a small boy, from the shop, holding my nose. It would take me years to realise how much and with what justification she had to complain about.

## MERTHYR TOWN CENTRE – CHINA

As Thomas Jones walked into Merthyr Tydfil at 1pm on Saturday, September 27, 1845 he could have been forgiven a smile of self-satisfaction. A moulder who manufactured expensive necessities out of cast metal – pipes, pans, wheels, complex pieces of machinery – he was a cut above your average ironworker. He was about to prove it.

With a swagger he wiped the dust off his jacket and walked into the Brecon Bank in the centre of Wales's first industrial town expanding more rapidly than any in Britain. He emerged with £200 burning a hole in his pocket.

It was an astonishing sum for a worker in the first half of the nineteenth century to withdraw in a single visit – four years' wages for the colliers who supplied coking coal to Merthyr's four giant ironworks. Perhaps Thomas, who lived at Aberdare five miles away, planned to buy property or start a business, or take a well-earned rest. First he craved a little excitement – a few beers, music, dancing, a flirtatious conversation or two with Merthyr's bar girls, famed for their wit if not their beauty. He called at the Globe, north of the Parish Church, and then the Crown, where Admiral Nelson stayed on his visit to Merthyr forty three years before. As night drew in, Thomas Jones started for home his money, minus a shilling or two, still tucked safely in his pocket. Time, perhaps, for one more drink in the cavernous Dynevor Arms which bordered China, as licentious and as dangerous as any a district in Britain.

More than 160 years after the moulder staggered towards his nemesis, a four lane highway drives through what was once the tangle of ironworks, tramroads, spoil tips, warehouses, evil-smelling tanneries, notorious public houses and alleys noxious with urine and raw sewage where industrial Merthyr was born. The River Taff still winds south of Cyfarthfa Castle and its park, past what was once the Cyfarthfa Ironworks before straightening under Jackson's Bridge to bisect the town. The bridge, once one of the busiest in Merthyr, choked with traffic and tramroads, now stands empty and forlorn, by-passed by the vehicles sweeping south through the town centre or west and north towards Swansea and Brecon. The Wellington, the last of the public houses that landmarked this part of Merthyr, flanks the bridge. Having set its face firmly against its raucous past, it is now a bright, upmarket Italian restaurant. South of the bridge, on the Taff's flat left bank, a terrace of pleasant houses, some hung with flower

baskets, now stands where once clustered brothels and dens of child thieves, money counterfeiters and receivers of stolen goods. The area had been mockingly dubbed 'China, The Celestial Empire,' by a glib-tongued journalist when the 1842 Opium Wars first revealed the splendours of that vast country to the gaze of the awe-struck British. The name stuck. The red light district extended north beyond Jackson's Bridge into Quarry Row and Caepantywyll and east beyond Bethesda Chapel into the slums of Newfoundland. To the south loured the huge Morlais Cinder Tip where the Penydarren Ironworks daily dumped its waste. To the west, 'Pontystorehouse' spanned the river and the Glamorgan Canal and lapped onto the Swansea Road on which stood the Dynevor Arms. But the heart of Merthyr's underworld beat in China.

Here you could find the 'Rodnies', gangs of rapacious child thieves and pickpockets operating under the supervision of Fagin-like gang masters. 'Rodney' would quickly pass into the Merthyr dialect as the generic term for a dirty, unruly child. Here, too, you found families of forgers with furnaces for the production of counterfeit coins set up in their kitchens. Here were the receivers ready to snap up stolen clothes and jewellery or even pots and pans at knockdown prices before selling them on. And here, most menacingly of all, you found the prostitutes, and their pimps and protectors. The women, most of them Welsh and sharing a handful of surnames took sobriquets to distinguish them from their fellow 'nymphs'. The nicknames were often triggered by incidents from their colourful pasts. Margaret Llewellyn became 'Peggy-two-constables', Maria Evans 'Bugle', and Jane Evans 'Dowlais Jane.' The women sold sex only as a last resort. Having lured their victims into their brothels their first plan was to rob them and let their 'bullies' toss them out into the street with volleys of kicks and threats.

It did not take long for two of Chinas nymphs' to spot Thomas Jones as a mark as he swayed up the Swansea Road towards the Dynevor Arms. Two walked either side of him, slipping their arms through his. Not surprisingly, perhaps, Thomas's account of what happened next as reported in the *Cardiff and Merthyr Guardian* is confused. He shakes off the two girls only to find them replaced by two more. He goes with them to the house of a notorious 'bully'. He takes a chair and they sit either side of him. To his horror he discovers half his money, in crisp white £5 notes, has disappeared. The girls deny his accusations of robbery. He rushes out shouting for help only to be bundled into the home of a second 'bully' who offers to help him get his money back. Instead, apparently reconciled to his loss, Thomas goes out and resumes his trek home. Once more he is accosted by two girls, one of whom was in the house when he lost his money. If he returns with them, they say, they will help him find it. They take him to the house of yet another 'bully' where he sits down, puts his hand in his pocket and pulls out the rest of his money still neatly pinned together. As he begins to count it, one of the girls snatches it and runs out into the night. When he rushes out to pursue her, poor Thomas is set upon by the 'bullies' and five or six others. His cries of "Murder! Murder!" bring help and he is led away and given a glass of the water he wishes he had stuck to earlier.

What strikes you about Thomas's account of the robbery is the cohesion Merthyr's 'Chinese' displayed in systematically relieving him of his fortune. The dozen or so involved in robbing him closed around him like the tentacles of an octopus. They used the weapons of entice-ment, intimidation, friendship, reassurance and physical assault with a skill a Guantanamo Bay interrogator would envy. China's sense of a community united against a hostile world was obvious at the Police Court hearing against those accused of robbing poor Thomas. The court room and the surrounding streets were packed with supporters of the accused who included 'Peggy-two-constables', 'Dowlais Jane' and their 'bullies' William Hudson and Edward Jenkins, alias 'Neddy Shon y Gôf.' Two were acquitted when Thomas Jones, perhaps intim-idated by the crowd, could not identify them. The case illustrates the chasm that yawned between China and the respectable world of the ironmasters and their workers. Yet when it came to fleecing its victims, Merthyr's underworld moved with a well-oiled precision those ironmasters could only envy.

## PENARTH, ST AUGUSTINE CHURCH – MERTHYR CHAPEL ROW

From the headland on which he sits he commands a breathtaking view. Two hundred feet below, Cardiff is laid out on its table-flat bay like a feast. Beyond the boats bobbing in the marina, past the ghost-like transparency of new Assembly Building, the squat, sleek Millennium Centre glints copper and gold in the late summer sun. Sweep left past the cranes, the towering flats and office blocks, and the Tongwynlais Gap spears north through the encircling hills to Merthyr and the Brecon Beacons. Castell Coch, a smudge of white against the grey-green mountain, flanks it. To the right, beyond the barrage and the long brown sandbanks burdened with factories, the gunmetal blue sea pads out into the Bristol Channel and beyond to Ireland and America. For more than a hundred years, the white marble pillar which marks Joseph Parry's grave has gazed out to the ocean, as if he is forever drawn from the land in which he was born to the land which made him.

The monument in the grounds of Penarth's St Augustine Church signals his importance. The narrow plinth is draped with a tasselled cloth carved in stone on which stands a sculpted lyre, symbol of the lyric poet as well as the musician. It befits the man still regarded as Wales's best composer, the creator of the iconic love song 'Myfanwy', and the hymn, 'Aberystwyth'. But if the grave, lovingly cared for by his admirers, celebrates his triumph, it also mourns his tragedies. It records his two sons, William Sterndale, dead at twenty and Joseph Haydn who died at twenty-nine as well as his wife Jane, who lived until 1918, surviving him by fifteen years. Parry was a man of headlong creativity, producing many hundreds of hymn tunes, oratorios and cantatas, not to mention nine full-length operas. Despite his walrus moustache, glasses and shock of white hair, he never lost his boyish looks or the irrepressible energy of the *enfant terrible*. His endless enthusiasm for life and for music, his naiveté and his appetite for public acclaim never waned. If he was envied and patronised by many in the Welsh academic establishment, the public adored him, labelling him 'Y Doctor Mawr', 'The Great Doctor', after he had completed his PhD in Music at Cambridge.

He was born in 1841 in Chapel Row, Merthyr Tydfil, thirty miles

north of his last resting place. His birthplace stood within the grounds of the Cyfarthfa Ironworks in which his father, Daniel, worked. His mother Elizabeth had been the servant of the minister at Bethesda Chapel, half a mile from the Parry home, a bastion of right-eousness against the lapping tide of unchristian China, with its nests of thieves, prostitutes and pimps, which bordered it to the south. Bet Parry was a

devout Christian and an accomplished contralto who often led the singing at Bethesda. Joseph, the third of her five surviving children, learned to love music at her knee. He became a leading alto in the chapel choir and a member of the famous choir led by Rosser Beynon.

There were more pressing preoccupations than music in his early years; helping the family to eat, for example. At nine he was already working twelve-hour shifts down a nearby mine for 2s and 6d (twelve and a half pence) a week. By twelve he was courting horrific injury working with molten iron as an assistant puddler at Cyfarthfa. In 1853 his father decided to emigrate to Danville, Pennsylvania where he took a job in the local ironworks. His family followed a year later and Joseph began work alongside his father. He started music lessons with teachers who were part of the Welsh-American community. His compositions hoovered up the prizes at local eisteddfodau. Encouraged, he submitted works to national eisteddfodau in Wales with similar success. At twenty he married Jane Thomas, the daughter of an immigrant from another South Wales iron town, Blaenavon. They would have five children. He spent three years studying at the Royal Academy in London and returned to Wales permanently in 1874 when he accepted the professorship of music at the new University College of Wales in Aberystwyth.

Parry never forgot his home town despite the fact that he never returned there to live. The pseudonym he attached to national eisteddfod entries read, 'Bachgen Bach o Ferthyr, eriod, eriod' – 'The little boy from Merthyr – always, always'.

The song for which he is still best-known may have been the product of that early life in the town. 'Myfanwy', published in 1875 when he was a successful, happily married man with a growing family, aches with the pain of first love:

> Paham mae dicter, O Myfanwy,
> Yn llenwi'th lygaid duon ddi?

A'th ruddiau tirion, O Myfanwy,
Heb wrido wrth fy ngweled i?
Pa le mae'r wen oedd ar dy wefus
Fu'n cynnau 'nghariad ffyddlon ffol?
Pa le mae sain dy eiriau melys,
Fu'n denu'n nghalon ar dy ol?

Why is it anger, Oh Myfanwy,
That fills your eyes so dark and clear?
Your gentle cheeks, O sweet Myfanwy,
Why blush they not when I draw near?
Where is the smile that once most tender
Kindled my love so fond, so true?
Where is the sound of your sweet words,
That drew my heart to follow you?

The song, many believe, was inspired by the boy Joseph's passion for the fiery and opinionated, but dutiful daughter of 'Blind Dick', a drunken former puddler, horribly injured in an accident at Cyfarthfa who was forced to wander the public houses of Merthyr singing for his supper. It is a satisfyingly romantic story, one which would have more credence if Parry had written the words as well as the music. In fact, 'Myfanwy''s Welsh verses are the work of the poet and lyricist, Richard Davies, 'Mynyddog', (1833-77).

Even though, on his return to Wales, Parry lived away from the town, first at Aberystwyth then at Penarth, he played a crucial part in the creation of a vibrant musical culture in Merthyr as an adjudica-tor, composer, and conductor of concerts. He wrote, for example, for the Cyfarthfa Band, founded around 1838 by Robert Thompson Crawshay. Nurtured with a parent's love by its founder, the band introduced the town to the best in contemporary music, through its arrange-ments of the works of leading operatic composers such as Rossini and Donizetti. Men like the composers and

conductors, Rosser Beynon and John Thomas, Ieuan Ddu, built on the foundations it laid. Later came the voluble, volatile choral conductor, Dan Davies, who managed to make mortal enemies in both towns by switching his allegiance from a leading choir in his native Dowlais to one in Merthyr. And there were important singers like another Dowlais man, Robert Rees, Eos Morlais, the 'Morlais Nightingale', whose fine tenor voice earned him a Wales-wide reputation. The great modern baritone Jason Howard, born in Twynyrodyn, Merthyr, has continued that tradition, earning international acclaim.

As Gareth Williams' fascinating history, *Valleys of Song*, graphically illustrates, the late nineteenth- early twentieth century was a time when Welsh musical culture flourished to the extent that major choirs enjoyed a support as intense as that commanded by the Welsh rugby side a century later. Fighting often broke out between rival supporters. If aggrieved fans felt an adjudicator had not been fair to their favourites, the poor judge would often need a police escort out of the concert hall.

If such passions had waned in the early twentieth century, Merthyr has continued to produce remarkable musical talent; among them Glynne Jones, another Dowlais man, the gifted conductor of the famous Pendyrus Male Choir. Glynne, who during his ten years as music master at the Merthyr County Grammar School turned the whole of that small school into a top quality choir, was yet another enfant terrible who shocked the town with his bohemianism and his homosexuality, and Wales with his attempts to shake it out of its hidebound traditions. He was as astonished as his critics when his campaign to have pop music performed at the national eisteddfod was accepted. It now flourishes there. It is yet another tribute to Merthyr's generosity of spirit as well as its pride in its achievements that a street in Dowlais has been named after Glynne.

Parry, too, inspired extreme reactions among his contemporaries as he does now among modern critics. If they are astonished by the fecundity of his imagination, they are often appalled by the fact that so much of what he produced is derivative and instantly forgettable. He lacked, they say, the discipline and the self-criticism which would have allowed him to reject the third-rate and concentrate on what was potentially first rate in his imagination. Often admiration and exasperation war within the same sentence. Gareth Williams sums him up, "[his] accessible tunes are sung a hundred years after his death and... the greatest Welsh composer remains Joseph Parry – alas."

## MERTHYR HIGH STREET – Y DIC PENDERYN

With its carpeted floors, its rows of polished dining tables, its walls clean of yellowing beer and tobacco stains and the varnish barely dry on its two-toned wooden bar, Y Dic Penderyn is an anachronism in the thinning ranks of Merthyr's public houses. Some reek with antiquity, like the Wyndham Arms around the corner in Glebeland Street, opened more than two hundred years ago when Merthyr was in the first explosive years of expansion from sleepy village to Wales's biggest industrial town. Castle Street, flanking Y Dic Penderyn, was in recent memory lined with hostelries, which grew up with the town in the days when their floors were laid with sawdust and harpists accompanied the songs and dances of drunken workers, assuaging thirsts created in hot furnaces and fetid underground tunnels. The Rainbow, the Beehive, the Lamb, the Parrott, the Patriot, the Walnut, the Iron Bridge; siren-like, they lured the world weary, the dupe and the young eager for shipwreck on the rocks of dissolution. Two in particular were focal points of the town's raucous social, cultural and

political life: the Beehive, famous for its women of the night – who also worked most of the day – and the black and white Lamb, home to poets, actors, journalists, teachers and manic patriots boasting of their membership of the Free Wales Army and their support for second home arsonists.

In stark contrast, Y Dic Penderyn's roots do not extend past a decade. It lacks the social cohesion of its predecessors. In

its spotless anonymity you are as likely to rub shoulders with a solic-
itor having lunch with a client as you are with the local drunk, a
dissolute journalist or an American tourist searching for his family
roots. But what the pub, curving around the corner of High Street
and Castle Street, lacks in personality it makes up for in historical
significance. It stands on the site of what was, according to historian
John Davies, the bloodiest and most ferocious industrial conflict in
British history. And according to fellow historian, Merthyr's home-
grown remembrancer, Gwyn Alf Williams, the rising of 1831 was
nothing less than an attempt at revolution. Triggered by a combination of desperate poverty, wage cuts, anger at the injustices of the
local debtors' court and demand for political reform, the uprising was
the moment when the working class emerged as a social and political
force in Wales, Professor Williams argues. It was the moment when
the Red Flag was first raised as a symbol of working class protest. It
produced that class's first and best-loved Welsh martyr.

Richard Lewis, Dic Penderyn, who has given his nickname to
Merthyr's newest pub, is an unlikely candidate for heroism. In the
words of Professor Williams, he personified the ordinary. He was the
typical 'face in the crowd'. Hardly anything about him beyond his
execution, on August 13, 1831 for his part in the uprising, and his
burial at Aberavon, is known with certainty. His admirers have
endlessly speculated over his character, his hatred of injustice, his
qualities of leadership. But their eulogies, unsupported by the facts,
smack of wishful thinking. He was probably born in Aberavon, was
called an ironstone miner at his trial and like his putative friend, Lewis
Lewis, 'Lewsyn Y Heliwr', probably alternated that with work as a
haulier. Richard was almost certainly married and lived alongside the
River Taff in one of Merthyr's most notorious working class districts.
He was probably just twenty three when he died, hanged at Cardiff
Gaol. And although he was the only rioter to pay the ultimate price,
the true leader was Lewsyn Yr Heliwr. It was Lewsyn who led the
crowd, probably ten thousand strong, which surged through the town
at the uprising's climax on June 3. He was in the van when they
besieged ironmasters, magistrates and prominent tradesmen sworn in
as special constables, who had gathered in the Castle Hotel opposite
what is now Y Dic Penderyn, on the spot where the Castle Cinema
stands. Defending the town's rulers was an eighty-strong detachment
of Argyll and Sutherland Highlanders hurriedly marched the eighteen
miles from their depot in Brecon. They were augmented by scores of
militia men. Lewsyn is said to have clambered up a lamp post to urge

the raging crowd on to confront the soldiers. He led them in their chants for 'Caws gyda bara', 'Cheese with (our) bread', symbolising their demand for something better than life on the breadline.

The numbers killed when the soldiers opened fire will never be accurately known. Friends and relatives stole bodies away and buried them in secret, fearing reprisals. But at least twenty-four protesters died and seventy were wounded. No soldier was killed, although eighteen were wounded, a third of them seriously. Among them was Donald Black, the young Highlander, stabbed by his own bayonet in the thigh after his rifle had been snatched from him. It was the act for which Dic Penderyn was hanged. But from the moment of his arrest, Merthyr's working people refused to accept his guilt – with good reason. He was convicted on the evidence of one man, the barber, James Abbott, an Englishmen who was in the hotel as a special constable as the mob besieged it. But Abbott admitted he spoke no Welsh and could not follow much of what was happening in the crowd. Dic claimed that Abbott hated him because they had fought during a demonstration for political reform in Merthyr the previous month. Witnesses corroborated their confrontation. Certainly, Professor Williams, after carefully sifting the available evidence, believes that Dic was innocent. It is a view his fellow citizens have eagerly endorsed for almost 180 years. As soon as he was dead Dic Penderyn passed into Merthyr's folk memory. His fate as a martyr and his example as a hero were passed from generation to generation around the family hearth. His last words as the hangman slipped the noose around his neck – "O Arglwydd, dyma gamwedd", "Oh Lord, here's injustice" – echoed down the years as a battle cry for the young in their own fight against injustice. Anything said to belong to Dic was treated with the piety given to the relics of Mediterranean saints. Professor Gwyn Alf Williams remembers his mother telling him about her grandmother who paid 4d to see what purported to be Dic's ear on display at Dowlais Market. That other great Dowlais historian, Sir Glanmor Williams, remembers in his autobiography his grandfather telling him as a little boy about Dic and the crime against him. "It was my first lesson in local social history," he says.

Gwyn Alf sees Dic Penderyn's ordinariness as the reason for the love and veneration his name still generates in Merthyr: "... it was not any leadership which made him a martyr; it was his very innocence, his innocuousness, his sense that he was 'only doing what thousands of others did'. The face of Dic Penderyn was the face in the crowd, the face the Merthyr working man chose as his own".

Even in a town which loudly celebrates its winners – epoch-making industrialists, poets, composers, newspaper tycoons, millionaire businessmen, doctors, politicians who change the world and historians who record those changes, boxing champions and footballers – the martyr has a special place in the hearts of a people who have never been strangers to suffering and injustice. After all, Merthyr is named after one, Tudful or Tydfil, the saintly daughter of the fifth century king Brychan, who died, perhaps defending her honour, at the hands of a band of barbarians marauding into Wales from Ireland.

## THE CASTLE CINEMA

Where once uniformed commissionaires greeted you as you walked up the shallow steps to a large and carpeted foyer, hung with the portraits of Hollywood stars, you now push through grubby swing doors to a claustrophobic cubby hole decorated with laminated wooden strips. The clack of falling skittles have replaced the cacophony of Indians chasing cowboys or the whispered endearments, magnified into ear-splitting stereophonic sound, of Clark Gable and Cary Cooper to Claudette Colbert and Grace Kelly. The Castle Cinema, once the finest art deco picture palace in the Valleys, has become a bowling alley, the latest of its many metamorphoses – bingo hall, nightclub, rock music venue, each a step down from its glamorous heyday.

Outside on a busy Thursday afternoon, traffic flows ceaselessly between the Castle and the decaying Old Town Hall. Inside, the soporific calm is broken only by the sound of a single ten-pin game. A café area of chairs and tables is deserted, as is the small bar and a coffee counter. Only the rake of the floor, where once tightly-packed rows of seats dipped down to the huge screen, suggests its past. A small video screen set in black now occupies the space once filled by its feature film predecessor. On the far wall, a handful of photographs and sketches of Marilyn Monroe, James Dean and Elvis Presley hint at past glories. Where tiers of balconies stretched to the distant roof, a low, pitch black false ceiling now presses down on you.

From the cinema's brightly-lit foyer with its ticket kiosk, its counters stuffed with chocolate bars, bags of sweets and popcorn you walked up to a maple-floored ballroom hung with more pictures of the stars. Doors off led to the curving mezzanine balcony, two intimate rows of seats stuffed with couples, each caught in a tangle of lips and knees and breasts as they groped for sensations more exciting than those promised by the screen. On the floor above stood the upstairs balcony, whose front rows offered the best seats in the house. Each programme contained two full length films and a variety of shorts. In the forties and early fifties, the interval between the 'A' and 'B' pictures offered more than a newsreel, a trailer or the stilted images and wooden commentary of a British film travelogue. A huge Christie electric organ, its fin-like side panels glowing with light, rose majestically from its pit in front of the screen like a Flash Gordon spaceship. Its steeply-tiered keyboards, art-deco seat and foot levers ribbed like the timbers of a sailing ship, piped out bright, rollicking marching tunes familiar to fans of radio's Reginald Dixon and his Blackpool Tower Organ. The Castle organ, one of the three best in Wales, had regularly starred in its own radio broadcasts before World War II.

A few years after that war, the Basini family would march up the steps of the Castle and into the foyer. It consisted of a father, 5ft 4ins and in his fifties, who had expanded into a plausible imitation of the Town Hall's square clock tower, a mother whose two sons, arriving

late, had left her as generously proportioned as an African earth goddess, and those sons, toddlers already filling out into the rugby prop forwards they would become. Ignoring the foyer's counters overflowing with chocolates and sweets – we had brought our own – we would march up the stairs towards the balconies. My father, with an immigrant's insouciant disregard for the customs of the natives, would lead us into the fetid darkness of the two-row mezzanine. As we settled into the front row, we began noisily munching through the mound of chocolate bars, sweets and biscuits my mother had taken from the shelves of our café and stuffed into her bag, as generously proportioned as she was. Behind us, the courting couples, having hastily separated as we rumbled in, resumed their quest for fulfilment, however transitory. Meanwhile on the screen the blonde, bawling Betty Hutton breathlessly hammed her way through the sharp-shooting title role of *Annie Get Your Gun*. Later, I would be part of the tide of howling children that flowed into the Castle on Saturday mornings for the ABC Minors' show which featured the likes of *Flash Gordon*, *The Lone Ranger*, *Abbot and Costello* and the *Bowery Boys*. Viewed now, the films are tawdry and amateurish, as exciting as day-long drizzle. Then, they enthralled me.

The Castle was merely the jewel in the crown of Merthyr's cinemas, which numbered eight or nine. Then there were none. After decades when fans had to travel to Aberdare, Cardiff or Newport to see a new film, at last we have the promise of a multi-screen. Like so many other buildings around it, the Castle is decaying. The storeys above the bowling alley are blocked off, their windows boarded up. Bushes grow out of the stonework. The stains left by cascading rainwater colour the walls. But in its comparatively short past as an industrial town, Merthyr has proved that, like almost everything else, history can be recycled. The cinema opened in 1929 on the site of a previous building that had been demolished to make way for it; not just any building, but one of the most significant, in a Merthyr awash with historical significance. A story more dramatic than any on the Castle's screen was played out here. The Castle Hotel was the focal point of the 1831 uprising, the moment when Merthyr's – and Wales's – working class was born. In a pitched battle, ablaze with gunfire and loud with the bloodcurdling slogans of revolt and the screams of the wounded and dying, the legend of Dic Penderyn was forged.

## MERTHYR HIGH STREET AND THE MINERS ARMS

At 9pm on a Friday, a walk the length of Merthyr High Street is edged with menace. The head-splitting jangle of Heavy Metal shreds the air from behind the crumbling façade of the Vulcan, where you and your Sixties friends crowded to gossip and drink to the songs of the Beatles. Framed in a window, a stick-thin girl, her eyes floating on a sea of black mascara, her denim skirt riding above grimy coloured stockings, buys a drink for her morose girl friend. A few doors away in the window of a Balti curry house, a couple pick at their food, feeding instead on their burgeoning quarrel. Two slab-like bouncers, primed for the night's violence, guard the entrance to a Wetherspoon's the size of a barn. Further north youths clutching their beer cans, gather around the memorial to Richard Trevithick to quarrel and jostle passers-by. Perhaps soon they will cross the road to inflict further damage on sculptor L.S. Merrifield's moving, vandalised war memorial. Children taunt the staff in Merthyr's best hotel metamorphosed into a Macdonald's. A hundred yards further into the maw of the nightmare more youths, unable to afford pub prices or to persuade even the most pliant barmen they are of age, splay across the road foaming beer from their cans. Their expletives bounce off each other like spent bullets: "Fucking cunt! Fuck off you fucking shithouse!"

I edge cautiously past.

Turn left past the squat, grey St David's Church and the bad dream turns gothic. Beyond the silver fluorescence of the light flooding from the giant 24-hour Tesco, the jagged remains of the Miners Hall, once a chapel, then a miner's institute, then a nightclub gutted by two fires, stand like the backcloth for a bleak Bronte romance. The hall, where fiery working classes orators like miners' leader A.J. Cook and the 'red' MP, Jimmy Maxton harangued their audiences to keep the socialist faith, is a roofless shell. Bushes thrust their tendrils through its lovely face. The rusting gates and battered ads for drinks and bar meals mock what is left of the building's dignity.

The side rooms, that once serviced the main hall with dressing rooms and rehearsal space, live on as a public house, the Miners Arms. Here, too, the music bounces off the walls and around your brain. The clipped vowels of Portuguese, pronounced as if through nostrils stuffed with cotton wool, mingle with the throatier Polish and Bulgarian.

A tiny bargirl, smiling constantly, slips effortlessly from her native Portuguese to English and back again. A handsome young Portuguese, muscles thickening under his tee-shirt, falls into the arms of a friend, a grey-haired Welshman. Two couples, their casually expensive clothes indicating they are strangers, sniff the atmosphere cautiously. They relax into laughter sensing, like me, that the town's drum-tight tension has now slackened into a welcome.

With a proper sense of history, what was once a focal point for Merthyr's socialism, the creed of international brotherhood, has become a meeting place for the latest wave of newcomers to a town built upon immigration. The Brazilians and their cousins the Portuguese, the Poles and the Bulgarians have added more layers to the tensile strength of a society formed out of the migrating Welsh, Irish, English, Spaniards, Italians, Russians, Chinese, European Jews, Indians and Bangladeshis. Some newcomers have earned themselves pivotal positions in the community, like Jose Pires, born in Tours in Northern France, the son of a Portuguese builder. He and his German wife, Marlies, arrived ten years ago to take over the Imperial Hotel at Pontmorlais, 200 yards from the Penydarren Park football ground and 100 yards from where novelist Jack Jones was born. He was working in a hotel in Slough, she for an airline when they met. Both were eager to start their own business.

Part of Merthyr's attraction lay in the fact that the imposing Imperial, with a rich social history – it was, as the Tiger Hotel, the headquarters of the newly-formed Merthyr Town football club one hundred years ago – was affordable. But the pair had the vision to see more than a business opportunity.

"We could see that Merthyr is a nice place to live. The countryside around here is beautiful."

He grins.

"And the fishing is terrific."

Under their management, the Imperial is remaking its reputation as a focal point for the town. Local societies have used it as their base, including the chess club. Groups of Welsh learners gather here to practice their language skills.

But most of the newcomers arrive to work in the meat packing plant that stands in the Dowlais Top trading estate, next to the Heads of the Valleys road. Once the plant, less than a decade old, imported most of its foreign workers from Portugal and Brazil. Now many come from the Eastern Europe. At night under its floodlights the factory appears a forbidding, prison-like place. But its workers have already added a splash of colour to Merthyr's streets. Lithe and beautiful men and women, often black, stride through the town with their mobile phones glued to their ears. Mothers, already thickening into Latin middle age, push prams through local supermarkets. The young cluster around the helpful and welcoming Central Library in Merthyr High Street, next to the Old Town Hall. The library's computer room has become a vital link with home. On a Saturday morning, it fills with Bulgarians, Portuguese or Poles eagerly email-ing friends and relatives.

The response to the newcomers is often hostile. "Bloody foreign-ers, taking over everything," a trader murmurs, quick to blame the town's ills, including drug trafficking, on them. But as the Miners Arms on this cold Friday night clearly indicates, knee-jerk reactions burn off in the cleansing forge of human contact. Mixed love affairs and marriages are increasing.

Help for the newcomers is extended through schools which appoint bilingual teaching assistants. The borough's library services hold inter-cultural evenings and English language classes. In a box on the corner of the bar in the Miners Arms stands the first edition of a free news letter produced by the University of Glamorgan. The glossy brochure is the product of the recently formed partnership between the university and Merthyr. The bulletin, in Polish as well as Portuguese, contains a welcome to the town, useful tips on visiting the doctor, facts about Merthyr. The town has, the brochure empha-sises, thrived on the arrival of foreigners. The staunchly Catholic Poles and Portuguese learn that the Irish established Merthyr's first Roman Catholic parish since the Reformation in 1815, that the town once had one of Wales's biggest communities of Jews, and that the Italians have been here for more than a hundred and fifty years. Merthyr's Italian community has produced the Bernis, founders of the Berni Inns; and, of course, Robert Sidoli, Welsh rugby interna-tional. Forget Merthyr's poets, priests, entrepreneurs and politicians, what better role model could an eager young Tomek or Paulo, or even Agata and Carla, strive to emulate?

## CENTRAL LIBRARY – ELIZABETHE CASIMIRO

Meeting Elizabethe Casimiro feels eerily like an encounter with my dead mother, when she first arrived in South Wales many years before I was born. Elizabethe, with a sallow Latin complexion, olive black eyes and a gentle smile, is a Brazilian of Italian extraction. She and her husband, Marcio, at thirty-six a year older than she is, are two of a growing number of immigrants who are putting down deep family roots in Merthyr.

In the seven years they have been here they have become leaders of their community. Marcio is part of the management team at the St Merryn meat packing plant on a spur of the retail park in Dowlais Top. Elizabethe works as a teaching assistant at a local school, where she helps immigrant Portuguese children to master English. She also helps adults to learn the language and to adjust to their new lives at classes run by the Workers Educational Association at the Dowlais Library.

She vividly remembers the problems she, her husband and their daughter, Samantha, twelve, faced when they first arrived in Merthyr less than a decade ago. They are those which must once have confronted the young Marina Basini when she arrived as a wild-eyed Italian peasant girl to join her brothers in the depressed Rhondda of the 1920s. For almost twenty years my mother helped run the family's half a dozen cafes, fish and chip shops and grocery stores before marrying my widower father and moving to Merthyr to raise his family and to start one of her own.

Elizabethe smiles wryly, perhaps amazed that she has survived, as she remembers her first days in a cold, grim South Wales town half a planet away from her home in southern Brazil. "At the beginning Merthyr was quite a shock for us," she recalls as we talk in an upstairs room of the graceful, grey-stone Carnegie Library in the town centre. "The culture, the people, the weather, the food, everything was just… so different. I said to myself, 'Oh my goodness! What am I doing

here?' It was difficult to adapt to a new life, a new language. The hardest part, for my husband as well as for me, was not speaking any English at all. That made it really difficult."

Instead of allowing her doubts and her fears to paralyse her, she met the challenge of a new life head-on. She immediately joined an English class at Merthyr College, now a part of the University of Glamorgan. Her husband, then working long hours on the production line of the St Merryn plant, was forced to take a more piecemeal approach to mastering the language: "He had to learn day by day as he went to work." Their daughter, Samantha, arrived to join her parents when she was just eight years old. She, too, did not speak a word of English. Now she happily devours a book in the children's library downstairs as her mother talks to me.

Natives like me complain endlessly about the amount of the town's priceless industrial past that has been lost beneath the demolition ball. But Elizabethe is impressed by the history she still sees around her. Her reaction probably owes much to the fact that she and Marcio come from a city the size of Cardiff which was still pasture land sixty years ago. Maringa, in the southern Brazilian state of Parana, close to the border with Argentina, has the look of a sprawling modern city with skyscrapers, plenty of green spaces and a futuristic cathedral resembling the Concorde's nose cone. Its 300,000 inhabitants live at the heart of a region whose chief economic activities are cattle-raising and coffee plantations.

Elizabethe's great-grandparents went to Brazil from Sicily and Parma, the province of Italy where the Basinis originated. They were drawn there by the shortage of labour on the coffee plantations created by the abolition of slavery. She was brought up on a farm outside the city before moving into Maringa to study for a degree in Education in its well-regarded university. She married Marcio, whose father is Portuguese, giving him dual nationality. When he was made redundant from his job as a tax inspector – "the Brazilians are as good at avoiding their taxes as the Italians" laughs Elizabethe – they first planned to find work in Portugal.

Then they met a friend, also of Portuguese extraction, who was already living and working in Merthyr. He had been found the job by an agency in Portugal which recruited workers for the St Merryn plant. "We thought it would be better to follow him to Merthyr because we knew there were jobs here and that there would be a place to live." She grins. "Merthyr is becoming famous in Maringa. Three of my husband's cousins as well as his friend have come here to work."

Marcio and Elizabethe first went to Lisbon to be recruited by the agency and to wait for documentation to be issued to them. She came to Merthyr in October, 2002, six months later than her husband. After a spell working on St Merryn's production line processing and packing meat, Marcio joined the management team responsible for quality control. He is now studying for an HNC in management.

They have bought a house in Upper Row, Penywern, yards from where the great historian, Gwyn Alf Williams, was born. As well as teaching them the language, the WEA classes at Dowlais Library help the immigrants to cope with the problems thrown up by their new life. Among them are finding suitable housing and job security. Workers from Poland and Bulgaria now outnumber the Portuguese at St Merryn. Like the Portuguese before them, the Eastern Europeans are on contracts for six months only when they first arrive.

She does not minimise the conflict between the immigrants and the natives. "We always have isolated cases of hostility, not because of race or nationality but because there are people who believe we are here to steal their jobs and their houses." That hostility has not prevented an increasing number of newcomers settling here. And, says Elizabethe, many immigrants are finding Welsh partners. "There are more mixed marriages now."

She worships alongside the Welsh at the Park Baptist Chapel near Penydarren Park. The resident ministers are husband-and-wife Brazilian missionaries. "The Baptists are strong in Brazil," she explains. She has to translate for those members of her congregation who do not speak Portuguese. Samantha goes to school at Bishop Hedley, the Roman Catholic comprehensive in Penydarren.

She and her family return to Brazil roughly every eighteen months for a holiday. But they have no plans to resettle there. "I love Merthyr and I have been very well accepted here. I have made lovely friends. Merthyr is a permanent part of my life now." Again her face breaks into a laugh. "I am even getting used to the weather – except for December and January when it is so dark and it rains so much. There is nothing like that in Brazil."

## THOMASTOWN – ST TYDFIL'S HOSPITAL

Even in bright spring sunshine, the crab-like cluster of grey-black buildings is grim and forbidding; something which would have delighted its creators. For, like the menacing Victorian prisons which dominate the centres of Cardiff and Swansea, it was built to warn people of the consequences of flouting society's rules. In the 150 years since they were opened the buildings have softened their impact. Their reincarnation as the St Tydfil's Hospital, in a hollow below Thomastown Park, has brought alterations and improvements.

Storeys and twentieth-century machinery such as lifts have been added. Lawns and broad access roads have been built and the hospital is flanked by a pleasant park. But enough of the original remains to induce a shudder of recognition in those who know its history.

This was once Merthyr's Union Workhouse, whose very name struck dread in the people who needed it the most, those threatened by homelessness and starvation. The Board of Guardians charged with running the workhouse encouraged that dread. In the proudly acquisitive world of the Victorians, being destitute was seen as a moral failing, much like being a thief. To discourage the 'undeserving poor', deemed by the Victorians to be sponging off the rest of society, conditions inside the workhouses had to be worse than those endured by the poorest labourer. The Guardians tackled the task of ensuring this with a will. The workhouse's formidable barricade of railings and its barred windows reminded the fearful population of a prison. The rules, too, had a strong suggestion of punishment through loss of liberty. Once inside its forbidding walls you were only allowed out if you undertook to leave permanently. Families were broken up as soon as they entered, wives separated from husbands, children from parents. All aspects of life inside were segregated. For a husband to cross the dining room to talk to his wife was a punishable offence, because it broke the rule of silence at mealtimes and because it was classed as fraternising with the opposite sex. The bell calling inmates to rise struck at 5am in summer months, two hours later in winter. Bedtime prayers were said at 8pm. Work routines, borrowed from prison, were often backbreaking and meaningless. Men were expected to break stones for eight hours a day or unpick oakum rope inch by inch. The ropes, often covered in tar, could shred a man's hands. Women were expected to do hard domestic work.

The diet was basic and meagre, consisting largely of rice, potatoes and bread. Watery soup was provided five days a week, small amounts of cooked meat – 4ozs for men, 3 1/2ozs for women – just three times a week. The only drink was water. Only the old were allowed a small ration of tea, sugar and butter. But perhaps the most damaging aspect of life in the workhouse was its sheer monotony. Children were not allowed the most basic toys. Those who ran the workhouse were often lax and neglectful. After one report into the badly run institution, the master and matron were persuaded to resign. Their successors were sacked barely a month later because of their drunkenness. The levels of poverty in Victorian and Edwardian Merthyr were so high that, despite its forbidding reputation, the workhouse was often full to overflowing. In 1909 for example, it had 655 inmates with bed space for only 500. The overflow had to sleep on the floor. Well into the twentieth century the workhouse retained its reputation as a place of punishment. As late as 1945, a girl of 13 was sentenced to spend twelve weeks there because she regularly ran away from home.

From the start, the workhouse had a small infirmary to care for sick paupers. Merthyr, with its epidemics of life-threatening diseases and its high-risk coal and steel industries, was woefully short of hospital beds. The infirmary was often pressed into service to treat the general population. Between 1890 and 1940, it was expanded and modernised. Imposing new buildings, some in a distinctive yellow brick, were added and after World War II it became the St Tydfil General Hospital. It is a place which had a special significance for my family. There my mother began her long fight with the illness that eventually killed her.

## TRAMROADSIDE CHOLERA CEMETERY

Lilac and white cherry blossom litter the soft-green lawn like confetti. A collar dove and two blackbirds grub for insects among yellow and purple flowers. The black-mesh, backless benches flanking the paths that weave through the trees are minimalist modern, but comfortable. Not even the compound of grey-black buildings, lowering above its screen of bushes like a storm cloud, disturbs the peace of this secret garden a hundred yards from the ceaseless din of Merthyr's High Street. Early on a fine spring morning, littered with birdsong, the sun warms this spot with the promise of new life. It was not always like this.

Less than thirty years ago, this little patch of Merthyr, on a plateau a few feet above Richard Trevithick's tramroad, yawned with crumbling tombstones like a mouthful of decaying teeth. Most told a story of suffering that, even in a town where terrible injury and a tormented death were as common as toothache, brought a shudder of horror to those who visited them. The cemetery had been attached to one of Merthyr's oldest chapels. It had opened in 1816 but, from the middle of the nineteenth century, it filled to overflowing with the victims of a pestilence that visited dirty, sinful, water-scarce Merthyr

like a biblical judgement. It was one of a pandora's box of diseases that scythed through the rat-infested hovels of a Merthyr where life was far cheaper than the expensive business of providing sanitation and a decent water supply. Habits such as throwing slops and the contents of chamber pots into the street, keeping pigs inside houses and defecating and urinating wherever the urge overtook you provided the environment in which disease flourished. Typhoid, dysentery, tuberculosis, scarlet fever and smallpox were some of the killers that decimated Merthyr's vulnerable population. So many infants died that life-expectancy in the 1850s was just 17.6 years. In some areas, including Dowlais and my own birthplace, Penydarren, it was less than 16. Tuberculosis caused at least one in five deaths while typhus, 'the Irish fever', accounted for one in nine.

But the disease which struck most terror into the hearts of the people first appeared in Wales in 1832. Asiatic cholera was a virulent bacterial infection of the intestines, causing intense diarrhoea and dehydration. It turned stools into a grey liquid flecked with chunks of bowel lining. Its victims rapidly became living corpses with hollow eyes, sunken cheeks and blue, puckered lips. The dying suffered extreme cramps and an insatiable desire for water. The disease arrived, like the medieval plague, in epidemics which swept through whole countries. It flourished in hot, dry summers. In 1832 it arrived first in North Wales, beginning with Flintshire on June 9. By June 24, it had reached South Wales, claiming victims in Newport, Swansea, Llanelli, Briton Ferry, Neath, Carmarthen, Builth, Margam and Aberavon. Merthyr topped the death toll with 160.

Seventeen years later, the scourge reappeared in the town, this time swelling in intensity until it killed ten times more people than that first epidemic. Notices appeared keeping a tally of victims and deaths in various districts of the twin towns of Merthyr and Dowlais. The epidemic began in May 1849 and by September 22 the clerk to the Board of Guardians reported that 1520 people had died. The eventual toll reached almost 1700. Ninety-three children died in the single Merthyr district of Georgetown. Cholera's victims included some of Merthyr's most important men, like Thomas Jones Dyke, the doctor who became the town's pioneering medical officer of health. He was ill for six weeks. But the vast majority of the victims came from the poor and the poorest of the poor, the Irish, suffered the most. In one later epidemic, 25 out of 30 who died were Irish.

When cholera struck, panic gripped the population, driving those who could afford it to leave and the rest into their chapels and churches. In the Merthyr courtroom, offenders paying fines had to throw their coins into a bowl of vinegar to disinfect them. In some families struck by the disease those unaffected departed, locking the houses behind them and leaving the sick inside to their fate. Windows had to be taken out to remove the corpses. At the height of the 1849 epidemic, burial grounds were so full that coffins were interred in only a few inches of soil, increasing the risk of polluting water sources. In Pant on the outskirts of Dowlais, a new cemetery was created to cope with the consequences of cholera. It is still in use. My parents and an elder brother are buried there.

The 1849 epidemic at last galvanised the town's elders into action. Fresh measures to clean up the filth in and around the streets were implemented, reservoirs built and a clean water supply piped to many

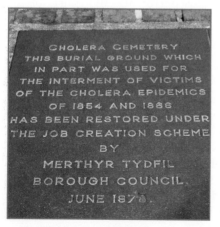

houses. New sewers were constructed. When cholera returned the measures were seen to be effective. An epidemic in 1854 killed 420, a fraction of those who died five years earlier. When the disease returned for three months in 1866, deaths fell to 119. So many of the victims of those last two epidemics found their way to the graveyard above Trevithick's tramroad, it became known as the Cholera

Cemetery. In 1975 Merthyr Borough Council cleared the tombs and employed a work experience team to build the park which flanks what was once Merthyr's Workhouse, now St Tydfil's Hospital. A plaque on a small red-brick plinth records its grim past. The park's beauty is an object lesson in the way even the most tragic piece of social history can be turned in to an environmental asset while retaining its historical significance.

## TWYNYRODYN – KEIR HARDIE ESTATE

These streets coiling crookedly around each other like a broken bedspring are a monument to Merthyr's political idealism. The increasingly privatised estate adds an architectural confusion to the drab grey pebble-dash that is the template of the town's council housing. Some homes have been modernised into log-cabin lookalikes with walls of dull-brown horizontal panels and triangular hoods over their front doors. Many retain the distinctive steel ribbing and the tubular steel porches of the prefabs, produced in their thousands in the euphoria of Hitler's defeat to usher in Britain's new dawn of social justice and a decent life for all.

The Keir Hardie Estate with more than three hundred houses, most of them prefabs, was Merthyr's first significant exercise in the provision of council houses after World War II. The borough councillors signalled their debt to the Labour politicians who had inspired them by naming its streets after them; Glasier Road, Dalton Close, Greenwood Close, Jowett Avenue, Wheatley Place, Wallhead Road. You need to be a serious student of twentieth century politics to identify the names. Only one, that of Aneurin Crescent, forming the outer coil of the spring, recalls a man well-known enough to give the layman a clue. It honours Aneurin Bevan, born ten miles away in Tredegar, the founder of the National Health Service and a key member of the post-war Attlee government which created the Welfare State

Other street names mark members of the Atlee government, such as Hugh Dalton, Chancellor of the Exchequer from 1947, and Baron Jowitt of Stevenage, Lord Chancellor and architect of Attlee's housing policy whose name is reflected in Jowett Avenue, despite its different spelling. Some honour Labour's founding fathers, like John Bruce Glasier, one of the four creators of the militant Independent Labour Party to which some of Merthyr's most influential councillors remained loyal, even after its acrimonious split with the Labour Party. Richard Collingham Wallhead, MP for Merthyr between 1922 and 1934 and chairman of the ILP between 1920 and 1923 is also celebrated. John Wheatley was a pioneer of council housing in the 1924 Labour Government. Above all, the estate commemorates the abrasive, passionate, lonely mystic and former Scottish miner, James Keir Hardie, the father of the Labour Party and Merthyr's first Labour MP between 1900 and his death in 1915.

The estate and its streets provide a graphic reminder of the stranglehold the Labour Party and its councillors have had on Merthyr politics since the 1920s. Its dominance of the local authority has been broken just once – in 1976 when Plaid Cymru gained control of the local authority and held it for three years. That period marked the high spot of the borough's disillusion with its Labour masters. The growing strength of that disillusionment had been evident six years earlier when Merthyr's much-loved MP, S.O. Davies who, despite his old-world courtesy and High Tory 'uniform' of black morning coat, waistcoat, striped grey trousers, homburg and white silk scarf, was an implacable left-wing rebel who delighted in challenging the conservatives within the Labour ranks. When the local party, its patience exhausted, finally rejected him as its candidate at the 1970 general election – officially on the grounds of his age, at least 84 – S.O. defied them and stood as an independent. Merthyr's youth, many of them socialists resentful of the political dinosaurs who ran the town, gathered around the sprightly old man. Their vibrant campaign coupled with the affection he inspired led to a remarkable victory.

What fuelled that profound disenchantment with Merthyr's Labour hegemony were the decades when the idealism and commitment to social justice evident in the building of the Keir Hardie Estate and the naming of its streets had solidified into what many of us saw as a reactionary conservatism buttressed by the party's dictatorship of the ballot box. "Put a donkey up in Labour colours and he'd win by a landslide" was the perpetual grumble. Too many local councillors acted as if they exercised the untrammelled power of dictators.

They could mould the lives of their constituents, doling out local authority jobs according to the politics of the applicants and the influence of their families. The teachers who poured off the educational production line discovered that without the right connections they were condemned to a life of exile in England or beyond.

My own rebellion had come a decade before that of S.O. and his army of young helpers. With a group of school friends in the late Fifties I founded a short-lived branch of the town's Young Conservatives. We lived up to the organisation's reputation for an active social life. We met every Friday in the upstairs rooms of the Merthyr Conservative Club to play table tennis and to dance before unleashing ourselves on the town's public houses beginning with The Eagle next door. But we did not neglect politics. I remember campaigning in the 1959 general election for an English barrister from the south east of England called Miranda Greenaway.

What I imagined the plum-vowelled Mrs Greenaway could give to the town I now have no idea. I still celebrate the values of the small businessman – among them, self-reliance and commitment to the family – I believed the Conservatives stood for. But after the holocaust of destruction visited on industrial South Wales by Margaret Thatcher twenty years later my youthful politics now seem to belong to another life.

I recognise that we owe the old Labour politicians we once purported to despise an enormous debt. They helped many of us grow up in relative comfort, free from the crippling effects of poverty. They gave us good schools, like mine at Cyfarthfa, and the means to go to university free from the money worries that plague today's generation. They fought enormous problems of financing to give those born into poverty the means to a better life through a reasonable health and welfare system and decent housing. And if some of the vast estates lacked necessary amenities such as shops and community centres, who could deny they were infinitely better places to live than the noisome slums of Caedraw or Dowlais?

But the enthusiasm of those post-war politicians for the heroes of socialism has been met with indifference by their ungrateful constituents. Most of those who grow up on the Keir Hardie Estate have no idea for whom their streets are named. Ask them where they come from and they will answer 'The Skeepo', a corruption of Yr Ysgubor Newydd, The New Barn, the name of the farm on whose fields the estate now stands. It is as if, in the community chosen to commemorate him, poor old Keir Hardie had never existed.

## CLARE STREET

In his gloomy, narrow-windowed study overlooking a dual carriage-way frantic with traffic he picked up a bright blue paperback and handed it to me shyly, his chocolate-brown eyes melting with pride. It was in a language I could not recognise – Swedish, perhaps, or Finnish. "See, Mario? Lots of countries are publishing my books now."

It was a moment of hubris the more startling from a man whose life epitomised a self-effacing devotion to literature. Amidst the quarrelling egos, the drunken sprees and the rhetorical excesses of his fellow writers, Glyn Jones was a focus of calm and a staid – some would say suffocating – respectability. Throughout his long life he remained loyal to the passionate, rigorous Christianity of his parents. His marriage to Doreen Jones, the daughter of a Cardiff business-man, lasted sixty years until his death at ninety in 1995. His career as poet, short-story writer, novelist and critic unfolded in tandem with forty years spent as a teacher, a profession to which, he freely confessed, he was never fully committed.

There was femininity in his narrow face lengthened by the high forehead, the large, liquid eyes and the thin, long-fingered hands. But his soft features masked an unbending morality some of his boister-ous fellow poets saw as a prim reluctance to engage with life, an arrogant judgement on their own behaviour. He struck an early friendship with his fellow poet Dylan Thomas, nine years his junior. They shared much, including family roots in the same part of Welsh-speaking west Wales and a lush, surreal use of the English language.

But Thomas felt threatened by the man in whom he saw the narrow Welsh values he had fought to shrug off. "He is a nice handsome man with no vices," Thomas wrote to his girlfriend, Pamela Hansford Johnson. "He neither smokes, drinks nor whores. He looks very nastily at me down his aristocratic nose if I have more than one Guinness at lunch." But however restrictive Glyn Jones's personal values may have appeared to some, nobody could doubt the courage with which he pursued them. His stance as a conscientious objector in World War II earned him persecution by the authorities and vilification by his fellow teachers.

He was, with the exception of Dylan Thomas and perhaps Jack Jones in his brief prime, the best of the Anglo-Welsh writers of his generation, a group which included the novelist and short-story writer Gwyn Jones and the versatile Gwyn Thomas. His professionalism made him a writer's writer, the obvious choice to lend his name to the offices of Academi, the body representing Welsh writers, at the Millennium Centre in Cardiff.

That equitable temperament helped him to play a key role in the formation and flowering of the Anglo-Welsh group in the decades straddling World War II. Immune to the petty jealousies and quarrels which so often poison relationships between writers, he became the group's fulcrum. The modest semi-detached house on Cardiff's Manor Way in which I interviewed him for the *Western Mail* in the late Eighties and which was his home for almost fifty years, was an open-house for writers and those interested in literature. Those who doubt his sense of humour had not listened to his waspish description of the unstoppable Gwyn Thomas, enthroned in his favourite chair in the Jones' living room, machine gun through an endless monologue while those gathered around, themselves never short of a word or three thousand, fought to get a syllable in edgeways. His lack of envy and malice made him a perceptive and generous, but honest, critic. *The Dragon Has Two Tongues*, a study of six of his fellow writers is an irresistible confection of autobiography, biography, anecdote and criticism, the best study of that first modern flowering of Welsh writing in English.

He spent seventy years in Cardiff, but the town which dominated his imagination was the Merthyr Tydfil into which he was born. He prided himself on the fact that he had never written a word which was not about Wales. And most of them were about Merthyr. It dominates his poems, many of his short stories and the novel often regarded as his masterpiece, *The Island of Apples*. Unlike Jack Jones, his friend and fellow Merthyr novelist who was the son of an impoverished miner, Glyn Jones was born into a genteel lower middle class. His father was a clerical worker in the Post Office, his mother, a red-haired beauty he was in awe of and intimidated by, a schoolteacher. While his father's family were immigrants from west Wales, his mother was that rarity, a descendent of the farmers who inhabited the Taff Valley before the arrival of the ironmasters. Both were Welsh-speakers, although the language of the home was English. Glyn had to fight to master the Welsh he sometimes wrote in. He said that he had missed becoming an entirely a Welsh language writer "by a hair's breadth".

He was born at 16 Clare Street on the southern fringe of Merthyr which runs parallel to the railway line to Cardiff. A bridge carrying that line stands at the street's entrance, its arches hosting a variety of businesses. A few hundred yards away on the main road is Hankey Terrace, a nondescript row of houses, each fronted by a patch of lawn, which forms part of the main street running south to Pentrebach and, eventually, to Cardiff. In 1912, it was the birthplace of another teacher turned internationally-known poet and short story writer, Leslie Norris. A plaque to his memory was recently unveiled in Merthyr's Central Library.

Glyn Jones tells us in a brief memoir written in Welsh and translated by Meic Stephens, that in the early years of the twentieth century when he was growing up there Clare Street was occupied by a colourful bunch of artisans and lower middle class professionals – a plasterer, a printer, a hay and corn merchant, a credit-draper, a binge drinking factory overseer and another famous son of Merthyr,

Arthur Horner, the communist and miners' leader who played a key role in the fight for a national miners union and in the establishment of the National Coal Board. The militant Horner was committed to another cause when he shared the street with the Jones. He was a Christian lay preacher. Clare Street remains a sturdily lower middle class terrace, the houses studded with double-glazed windows, lantern porch lights and satellite dishes.

A chasm yawns between Glyn Jones the man and his work. The balanced, eminently sensible schoolteacher harbours an unruly imagination whose images of death, corruption and decay erupt on to the page. *The Island of Apples* purports to be a gentle rite of passage, a boy's journey from the golden innocence of childhood to the darkening world of the adult. Yet, like a Grimm's fairytale, it seethes with violence, murder and mayhem. Almost without exception the adults are grotesques whose stumpy bodies, rotund faces livid with ugliness or grossly fat frames symbolise their drunkenness, greed and lack of moral and intellectual stature. Only one character, apart from the hero-narrator, seems to escape the author's vengeful judgement, the idealised Karl Anthony. And he lacks the energy and the subtlety to convince us he is anything but a cypher.

Nightmarish themes burst free of naturalistic restraint in a story like 'Jordan', which begins as a humorous study of a pair of rogue salesmen conning their way through the fairs of South Wales and quickly darkens into a tale of body snatching and zombies. Its central character, the eponymous doctor's servant, is a monster as terrifying as Frankenstein but with none of the latter's humanity. 'I was born in the Ystrad Valley', a haunting fantasy of terrorism and revolution set in a fictionalised Merthyr Valley, ends with its fugitive hero literally transformed into the rock, the grass, the crags and summits of the mountain on which he has taken refuge.

Like Wyn, the hero of that story, Glyn Jones's own sense of psychic integrity appears thin and fragile, all too easily overwhelmed by the darkly chaotic contents of his subconscious mind. It is as if the persona of the equitable schoolteacher is a construct to protect the writer from the terrors of his own imagination. Or perhaps the mildness of the man acts as a conduit along which the power of the writer's subconscious can more easily travel. Either way, as readers we can only be grateful.

## MOUNT PLEASANT – MERTHYR VALE

This is a land contoured by loss. Two miles from the flattened waste tips, the cemetery's pristine order, the memorial garden bedraggled in the driving rain and the endless remembering of Aberfan, a spatter of houses testifies to a tragedy smaller but of great significance: a legalised murder whose injustice helped to make British law less barbaric. The short street sheaths what was once the main road to Cardiff. Its eastern terrace is a sliver of houses sandwiched between the mountain and the road cut into its flank. Steps rise steeply from the kerb to patches of garden and damp, drab extensions. To the west where the ridge falls sharply to the valley floor, the houses cling to the road like petrified climbers. The street sign reads 'Bryn Hyfred', 'Mount Pleasant', and so it is, with the purple-heathered mountain rising steeply at its back and the jagged beauty of the ridge across the valley, bare and burnt brown above the plastic-green pines.

Timothy John Evans was born here almost eighty-four years ago. He was the unlikeliest tragic hero. From the first, his life seemed destined for insignificance. Thin, long-faced and frail with black hair and eyes like nuggets of coal, he stood less than 5ft 6ins tall and weighed under ten stone. He was variously described as "a funny little chap" and a "little runt of a man" by his contemporaries. Nature signally failed to compensate for his physical frailties with intellectual brilliance. In 1949, when he was twenty-four years old, he was found to have an IQ of a boy of ten. He did not begin to speak until he was five years old. He had had virtually no education in the village school which stills stands, its white walls edged with red brick. It shares the valley floor with the main Merthyr to Cardiff railway line, a housing estate and the River Taff. Playing as an eight year-old in the river Evans cut his right foot badly on a piece of glass. The wound developed a tubercular sore which never properly healed. He spent much of the next decade in hospital and walked with a limp for the rest of his short life.

As if all that was not enough,

his father, like almost every other man in the area a miner at the Merthyr Vale Colliery, had abandoned his family when Timothy was still in the womb. His mother married again and in 1935 when her son was eleven, the family moved to London to escape the Depression. Evans's stepfather, Penry Probert, managed to find a job as a painter and decorator. In 1937, still undergoing extensive hospital treatment, Evans returned to Mount Pleasant to live with his grandmother. By 1939 he was back in London. He would continue to use Mount Pleasant as a bolt hole when trouble threatened. Having formally left school, Evans set about proving he was not without resources. He was, despite his lack of measurable intelligence, rich in imagination and a great spinner of tales, many of them about himself. He told people he was the son of an Italian count. Although he could not read, he held down a job as a van driver, delivering all over the south of England. Attractive to women, he married the pretty but feckless eighteen year-old Beryl Thorley in September, 1947. When the couple moved into a flat in seedy, rundown 10 Rillington Place, Notting Hill, they sealed their tragic fate. Below them lived the bald, owlish John Reginald Christie, forty-nine years old but looking a decade older, outwardly a pillar of respectability with an enviable record as a special constable during World War II. He would, within a few years, be unmasked as perhaps the most notorious serial killer of the twentieth century.

Timothy and Beryl had a daughter, Geraldine, in October 1948, a few months after they had moved into Rillington Place. When Beryl found herself pregnant again, she could not face the prospect of feeding another mouth on her husband's meagre pay. She went to

Christie who claimed a talent as an abortionist. When Evans returned from work the day of her supposed abortion, Christie told him she had died during it. Having been assured by Christie that he would dispose of Beryl's body "down the drains" and would send Geraldine, now a year old, to stay with friends, Evans escaped to Mount Pleasant to stay with his aunt and uncle. On November 30, at Merthyr

Vale police station, a mile from his relatives' home, he told a detective sergeant that Beryl had died after taking abortion pills he had found for her. He had, he said, put her body down the drain outside 10 Rillington Place. A police search of the drains found nothing. Evans made a second statement, this time revealing Christie's role in his wife's death. When the bodies of Beryl and Geraldine were eventually discovered hidden in a washhouse at the back of 10 Rillington Place, Evans was taken to the Notting Hill police station where he made two more statements, this time saying he had strangled both Beryl and Geraldine. Evans was tried for the murder of Geraldine, found guilty and hanged on March 9, 1950. He was twenty-five.

Three years later, the remains of half a dozen women, including three prostitutes and Christie's wife, were found in the garden of 10 Rillington Place and in Christie's flat. The mild-mannered, monstrous, Christie had killed them for sexual gratification, having intercourse with them after they were dead. Christie confessed to the murder of Beryl Evans and indicated he may have killed Geraldine. Convicted of the murder of his wife, Christie was in turn hanged on July 15, 1953. The Conservative government, anxious to respond to the mounting concern that Evans had been hanged for a crime he had not committed, hastily set up an inquiry led by the Recorder for Portsmouth, John Scott Henderson QC. Amidst a clamour of disbelief, often loudest from MPs, he found that Evans was guilty.

In his examination of the case, published in the book *Ten Rillington Place* in 1961, the journalist Ludovic Kennedy unveiled a devastating analysis of how the innocent Evans had been convicted. Kennedy pointed to the similarities in the way Beryl Evans and the rest of Christie's victims had died. He condemned the police investigation for ignoring evidence that favoured Evans. He cast massive doubts on the 'confessions' extracted from Evans at Notting Hill, alleging the hapless Welshman had been 'fitted up' by police certain of his guilt and not prepared to let the lack of evidence stand in their way.

Kennedy highlighted flaws in the way the defence and prosecution at Evans's trial had been conducted and condemned the 'gross distortion' of the truth contained in the judge's summing up. His book also condemned the methods and the conclusions of Scott Henderson's quick-fire review of the case.

Astonishingly, a second review conducted by Judge Daniel Brabin after the publication of Kennedy's book also concluded that although he probably did not kill his daughter, Evans probably did kill his wife. Both reviews indicated just how difficult it was for the British legal establishment to admit it had killed an innocent man. It was not the only time the British Establishment closed ranks to protect its own in the Fifties and Sixties.

Brabin's report was published on 12 October, 1966, just nine days before Tip No 7, high above Aberfan and just up the valley from Timothy Evans's birthplace, collapsed and flowed down the mountainside to engulf Pantglas Junior School. One hundred and sixteen children and twenty-eight adults died. The Labour Government, led by Harold Wilson, refused to put the blame for the Aberfan Disaster where it belonged – on the men who ran the National Coal Board and, in particular, on its chairman, the arrogant Lord Robens.

But the tragic death of Timothy Evans did have a positive outcome. After Brabins's report clearing him of the murder of his daughter, Evans was given a posthumous free pardon. The case had already played a vital part in discrediting capital punishment. In 1965, Parliament, led by the reforming Home Secretary, Roy Jenkins, suspended the death penalty for five years. It was abolished in 1969.

## ABERFAN

Beneath the dazzling glare of floodlights that turned night into day an army of rescuers scurried and picked and dug over the mountain of thick, black, evil-smelling sludge. The shifting ooze beneath their feet sucked them in to their ankles, rotting the leather of their boots and shoes as if it was cardboard. Human chains, along which buckets of mire passed to the line of waiting lorries, snaked down the mountain that now stood where hours before there had been houses and schools and the excited chatter of children. Bands of volunteers from the Salvation Army, the Women's Royal Voluntary Service, the Red Cross and the St John's Ambulance offered the rescuers an endless supply of sandwiches and hot, sweet tea from mobile canteens, the backs of vans or trays slung, like those of cinema usherettes, around their necks.

At intervals a long shrill blast on a whistle brought a breath-held silence to the clatter of shovels and picks and the muted chatter. All eyes turned to the Pantglas Junior School that had been engulfed by the roaring avalanche spewed out by the tip, suspended like a giant Sword of Damocles above the village of Aberfan. Ears strained for a cry, a sigh, a whimper that might signify life beneath the chaos of mud, collapsed walls, twisted wood, broken glass, buckled rails and coal trucks that had been tossed like foam on the tidal wave of slurry. It was, the rescuers knew, a forlorn hope. The last child taken alive out of the school had been many hours before at 11am, ninety minutes after the towering wall of slime had buried it. But it was that hope, sustained in defiance of the facts, which fuelled their heroic determination. And long after the hope had finally faded, when they knew the best they could hope for was to turn tenderly uncovered bodies over to grieving parents, they worked on.

Ask me what I was doing when J.F. Kennedy was assassinated in 1963 and I have no idea. I have only the vaguest memories of watching the flickering television images of man first walking on the moon. But almost every moment of Friday, October 21, 1966 is etched in acid on my memory. I was a student in Cardiff. Having spent a year teaching after I had left Aberystwyth, I had returned to university, ostensibly to obtain a Certificate of Education. But I had already decided teaching was not for me. I needed time to work out what I really wanted to do with my life.

I was staying with relatives and I had no plans to return to Merthyr that weekend. I saw the first vague reports of a disaster at Aberfan on television. As the morning unfolded, the number of smudged grey pictures from the village increased. With each report the hysteria of the reporters, panicked by the scale of the disaster confronting them, became shriller. By early afternoon it was obvious a tragedy unprece-

dented even in a Merthyr inured to death on an industrial scale was unfolding. I decided, along with thousands of Merthyr people from around Britain and the globe, that I had to go home. I had none of the skills needed to help in the rescue. The television reports had long since spelled out the main problem facing the stricken village; too many inexperienced volunteers cluttered up approach roads and hampered the efforts of experts. But I had to be home in that desperate hour.

That evening my brother and I put on some old clothes and drove to Aberfan. We joined a human chain, passing endless buckets of slime from hand to hand down the line. We stayed for several hours before handing our places to others, just as eager to assuage their need to do something, anything, to help. My involvement in the tragedy of Aberfan was brief and comparatively pain-free. For my closest friend the disaster meant a descent into hell. It became a personal tragedy that has haunted him for four decades since.

Mansel Aylward was twenty-three and close to qualification as a doctor when on that Friday in late October 1966 he and wife, Angela, left London with their eighteen month-old son, Simon, for a weekend home in Merthyr. They had set out before dawn since the journey in their small Ford Poplar was long and tiring in those pre-M4 days. By around 10.30am they reached the outskirts of Dowlais. A policeman stopped them just as they were about to go down through Dowlais and Penydarren and into Merthyr to Angela's family home in the Brecon Road.

"What's the trouble?" Mansel asked.

"There's been a disaster in Aberfan," the policeman replied.

The news was particularly disturbing since Mansel's father had been born in the village, five miles south of Merthyr. Close relatives still lived there.

"I thought, 'Oh my God, the pit has gone'," he remembers.

They were trying, the policeman said, to keep main roads into Merthyr free for the ambulances ferrying the injured to the town's

hospitals. Instead, the Aylwards would have to use the Slip Road which skirted Merthyr. Then he noticed the badge on the car indicating Mansel was a member of the British Medical Students' Association.

"I'm not yet qualified," Mansel explained.

"You could still be useful," replied the policeman. "You should go down there to see if you can help."

He allowed Mansel to travel into Merthyr to drop Angela and the baby off before leaving for Aberfan. As Mansel approached the village he still believed the disaster involved the Merthyr Vale Colliery, whose waste had been stored in the seven tips on the mountainside above Aberfan. Half a mile from the Mackintosh Hotel, which stood in the centre of Aberfan close to the stricken school, he was astonished to see the oozing river of slurry and rubble blocking the road. Policeman and rescuers stopped him.

He was told to park the car and walk the rest of the way.

"All I could see was this awful mud. Nobody had told me what had happened. I told them who I was and that I had not yet qualified. They told me it did not matter since there were only two or three doctors there."

The rest, he was told, were at Merthyr's hospitals, expecting an influx of survivors. There were none. By the time he got there the last survivor had already been taken from Pantglas Junior, which had borne the brunt of the avalanche, and Pantglas Secondary School, a few doors away. Instead of offering succour to injured miners, the young medical student found himself digging the bodies of children and their teachers out of the classrooms in which they had died.

"All these children were dead. Nobody alive at all. And we found the teachers where they had died, trying to protect them.... "

Professor Mansel Aylward CB, former chief medical adviser to the Department for Works and Pensions, Chairman of the Wales Centre for Health, director of the Centre for Psychosocial and Disability Research at Cardiff University, visiting professor at Harvard University, breaks off, his voice cracking under the strain of reliving hellish memories.

There were already lots of rescuers and some miners. "But nobody seemed to know what to do. It was chaos."

Order would come later, he recalls, with the arrival of the miners' rescue team and army sappers. He remembers his guilty relief when he was finally called away from the digging to exercise his medical skills. He was needed to treat rescuers who, never having used picks

and shovels before in their lives, were succumbing to the hard physical work with a variety of ailments ranging from strained backs and chest pains to full-blown heart attacks. The waiting ambulances finally had their cargoes to rush to hospital.

That night and the following day, Mansel accompanied members of the Salvation Army as they visited stricken parents and escorted them to the temporary morgue in Bethania Chapel where the bodies were laid out on pews beneath blankets. Now he and his fellow rescuers found themselves besieged by the world's media, demanding interviews and photographs.

It was only when he snatched time for a visit to relatives that he realised how closely the tragedy had touched him. His nine year-old cousin had died in the junior school. Another had a miraculous escape when she had been sent home from the school to fetch a bag of sugar. The avalanche struck minutes later.

He was at Aberfan for two days without a break, snatching the odd hour of sleep. He remembers his exhaustion and his dream-like emotional detachment. It was not until he went home to his family in Merthyr that the unstoppable tears began. He returned to Aberfan once more for the impressive mass funeral when the mourners shuffled in an unbroken line from the hillside cemetery down through the village. And he attended the individual burial of his cousin.

For decades, every October 21 or when television programmes and articles recalled the disaster, Mansel Aylward found himself reliving those terrible days. "I would dream of digging into that classroom, of finding the children and laying them out. I would relive the moment again and again."

The Aberfan Disaster, triggered by the arrogance and incompetence of those at the top of the National Coal Board, its effect on the community compounded by a Labour government in thrall to the board's overbearing chairman, cost one hundred and forty-four lives. One hundred and sixteen of them were children, mostly aged between seven and eleven.

My own involvement with Aberfan continued. On major anniversaries I would return to the village to research long newspaper articles. It was a job I hated. I could never rid myself of the feeling that I was intruding on a very personal tragedy. I felt that what I and legions of other journalists, and even the social workers who ministered to the needs of the stricken families, were doing was to prolong the mourning process, never allowing the wounds to heal. Perhaps I was wrong. Perhaps I underestimated the depth of the trauma. The wounds would never heal. All Aberfan could hope for was to live with them. For that it needed the support of those who ministered to them and the sympathy of a world reminded of their plight by the writers, photographers and broadcasters who returned there.

The articles and television programmes recreating those terrible events not only remind us of the price the Valleys have paid for making their meagre living out of coal and steel. They pay tribute to the courage of villagers who took responsibility for their lives and for the recovery of their community. And they recall the betrayal of that community by those they trusted, by a Labour government and its creature, the National Coal Board, both of which Aberfan had served loyally and too well.

# CENTRAL 2

## PENYDARREN SOCIAL CLUB

Midnight. The New Year. Women parcelled in paper hats and ribbons of tinsel jostle through the cavernous concert hall and side bars showering kisses like confetti. Their beer-bellied fathers, husbands and boyfriends, loud in bright shirts and silver ear rings, grumble each other a swift greeting and down another pint. Billy Piper, a pensioner with an ear-ring and the tight, taut body of a lightweight boxer, turns, pulls up his shirt and for the umpteenth time shows admirers his Christmas present to himself, the badge of his beloved Liverpool Football Club newly tattooed across his back. In the carpeted lounge, a hospital doctor with an English accent wishes the mayor, Allan Jones, celebrating the festival with his family, a success-ful New Year.

The Penydarren Social Club is barely thirty years old. But no-one, least of all the devotees who crowd it tonight, would claim it repre-sents the cutting edge of architectural or cultural style. The flat-roofed, single-storied, barrack-like square of purple bricks defines functional ugliness. The highlight of the evening concert in the packed hall is a band bellowing out 'Ticket to Ride'. And yet for more than thirty years it has represented the hopes and aspirations of the streets which spawned it. Without it Penydarren, one of the liveli-est, funniest and most rewarding of the communities that make up Merthyr's rich human heritage would probably not have survived.

At the start of the Seventies the rise on which the club stands overlooked the High Street, the heart of Penydarren's self-contained world. The street pumped out its commercial lifeblood to the rest of the village built on the steep ridge rising from Merthyr to Dowlais.

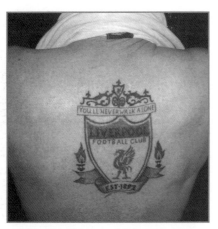

The society that grew on the High Street was one of Merthyr's oldest. It had been born in the mid eighteenth century along with the Penydarren Ironworks, which once stood in the broad hollow below the High Street, two hundred yards from the Penydarren Club. It was a homogenous society despite its extremes of abject poverty and middle class comfort. It spawned characters like tall, flagpole-thin Johnny Donovan, a would-be street entertainer, dressed in tails and white daps, white shirt, bow tie and a buttonhole in his lapel. He would have been immaculate except that the shirt was filthy, the gym shoes grime-covered and full of holes, the torn suit stiff with dirt. His efforts to entertain were thwarted by the fact that, ninety per cent of the time he spoke a gibberish making sense only to him. Johnny, like many others, was never spurned or merely tolerated. He was cared for, bought meals, offered shelter. His survival symbolised the generosity which is the true yardstick of community.

The cradles of Penydarren's community were the nine public houses that lined the High Street and the streets parallel to it. Each was its own universe. Each commanded a loyalty broken only in the most extreme circumstances: a change of landlord, a quarrel with a friend, the souring of the beer, the arrival of interior decorators about to transform the place. Customers would be labelled a 'New Inn Man' or 'Rose and Crown all his life'. My father, dead thirty years, is still known as a 'Crystal Palace man.' Then came the decision to run a new road through Penydarren. It would mean the destruction of the High Street and several streets running parallel to it. The shops, the chapels, the cafés, would go. So would the public houses except for the Norton. The social and cultural, as well as the commercial, heart was about to be torn out of Penydarren.

It was not a situation the village was prepared to tolerate. A group of men from my father's pub, the Crystal Place, including accountant Doug Evans and a steelworks executive, the late Des Thomas, got together. They toured Penydarren's about-to-disappear pubs trawling for three hundred people prepared to stake £1 each on the future, on funding a new social framework, and found them with little difficulty. They formed a committee drawing on the village's deep well of talent: a buyer for the Hoover washing machine factory, a key local government officer, men with contacts in the building industry.

When their first idea, a community centre with bars, fell through they turned to Plan B, building a social club. A Cardiff builder prepared to construct the club found them a brewery willing to finance it. It was an idea fraught with financial risk for the committee and its trustees. The Penydarren Social Club opened in 1977 and, as I witnessed on that New Year's Eve in 2007, flourishes. Its success is measured in more than the size of its membership. It draws families, long exiled by redevelopment and the search for jobs to other parts of Merthyr and beyond, back to drink in its halls and bars and to reminisce with friends and relatives.

Merthyr, critics argue, is a town burdened by its sense of history. It is still possible to find locals buttonholing strangers to lecture them on the town's remarkable past, still possible to visit a pub and be told by a young mother with ringing if inaccurate certainty that that Merthyr "was once the capital of Wales, you know. Everything happened here." She bristles with indignation when she recalls that in 1939, long before she was born, a remote London think tank, Political and Economic Planning, recommended that Merthyr, gripped by the Depression, should be abandoned and its population shipped down to the coast. The positive side of that obsession with the past is the sense of belonging, of identification with a massive extended family. That sense of community is embodied in the Penydarren Club

The town is beset by problems, such as its polarisation into a society of haves, the commuters in brand-new private estates living cheek-by-jowl with the have-nots, the unemployed condemned to life without much hope on their sprawling council estates. Among the former the situation breeds a nervous superiority, among the latter, a sense of hopeless exclusion and a dangerous resentment. Merthyr continues to top all the wrong leagues: poverty, ill-health, unemployment. Drugs, alcohol and the crimes they spawn feed on the people. The local authority, which has too often wilted in the face of the massive problem of how to preserve the evidence of Merthyr's past, is already grappling with its biggest heritage headache – how to save the visibly ageing Cyfarthfa Castle for posterity.

There are signs of hope. Imaginative initiatives might yet save more of Merthyr's threatened buildings as one appears to have saved the iconic Old Town Hall, now the headquarters of a Merthyr Housing Association bubbling with plans to restore it to its former splendour. A new complex at Rhydycar near the town centre includes a leisure centre, a multi-screen cinema, a bowling alley, a hotel and no less than three swimming pools. Several retail parks have opened or are under construction. The Welsh Assembly Government's impressive new office block close at Rhydycar has brought five hundred jobs with it. A business and innovation centre is being built next door. New industry, including a mobile phone call centre and a meat packing plant, has arrived in recent years. The University of Glamorgan's fruitful partnership with the town may result in a brand-new life-long learning campus with an arts centre. Merthyr's most visible asset, Cyfarthfa Park and its castle, will form part of a £12m tourist development undertaken jointly by the Welsh Assembly and Heads of the Valleys local authorities. The park, home to a successful Donny Osmond concert in 2007, will become 'an activities and events' venue.

But the true hope for a better future for the town which pioneered modern Wales lies in its people, like those of Penydarren who, threatened with extinction, discovered in themselves the resilience and the talents needed to remake their community.

# THE PHOTOGRAPHS

# WORKS CONSULTED

Aberfan and Merthyr Vale Community Co-operative *Aberfan Our Hiraeth, Aberfan and Merthyr Vale Community Co-operative*, 1999.

Austin, Tony, *Aberfan The Story of a Disaster*, Hutchinson, 1967.

Borrow, George, *Wild Wales*, Gomer Press, 1995.

Broadbent, Rick, *The Big If, The Life and Death of Johnny Owen*, Macmillan, 2006.

Burton, Anthony, *Richard Trevithick, Giant of Steam*, Aurum Press, 2000.

Carter, H. and Wheatley, S., *Merthyr Tydfil in 1851: A study of the Spatial Structure of a Welsh Industrial Town*, University of Wales Press, 1982.

Clarke, T. E., A *Guide to Merthyr Tydfil*, published 1848, reprinted Cardiff Academic Press, 1996.

Colpi, Terri, *The Italian Factor, The Italian Community in Great Britain*, Mainstream, 1991.

Croll, Andy, *Civilizing The Urban, Popular Culture and Public Space in Merthyr, c. 1870-1914*, University of Wales Press, 2000.

Davies, James A., *Leslie Norris, Writers of Wales series*, University of Wales Press, 1991.

Davies, John, *A History of Wales, Revised Edition*, Penguin, 2007.

Davies, John, *A Pocket History of Cardiff*, University of Wales Press and The Western Mail, 2002.

Davies, Russell, *Hope and Heartbreak, A Social History of Wales the Welsh, 1776-1871*, University of Wales Press, 2005.

Defoe, Daniel, *A Tour Through the Whole Island of Britain, Vol 1, 1724*.

Eagan, David, *Coal Society, A History of the South Wales Mining Valleys, 1840-1980*, Gomer Press, 1982.

Eagan, David, *People, Protest and Politics, Case Studies in 19th Century Wales*, Gomer Press, 1982

*Early Industrial Merthyr Tydfil*, University of Wales Press, 1993.

Edge, David, *Abergavenny to Merthyr, Country Railway Routes*, Middleton Press, 2002.

Evans, Chris, *The Labyrinth of Flames, Work and Social Conflict in Early Industrial Merthyr Tydfil*, University of Wales Press, 1993.

Evans, E.A. *Over the Top to Dowlais, Steam Days No 56*, p 238, April 1994.

Ferris, Paul, edit., *The Collected Letters of Dylan Thomas*, Dent, 1985.

Griffiths, Robert, *S. O. Davies*, Gomer, 1983.

Gross, Joseph, edit., *The Diary of Charles Wood of Cyfarthfa Ironworks, 1766-1767*, Merton Priory Press, 2001.

Guest, Revel, and John, Angela V, *Lady Charlotte, A Biography of the 19th Century*, Weidenfeld and Nicolson, 1989.

Hart-Davies, Duff, *The House The Berrys Built*, Hodder and Stoughton, 1990.

Hayman, Richard, *Working Iron in Merthyr Tydfil*, Merthyr Tydfil Heritage Trust.

Hughes, Brian, *Reaching for the Stars, The Howard Winstone Phenomenon*, Collyhurst and Moston Lads' Club, 2005.

Hughes, Colin, *Lime, Lemon and Sarsaparilla, The Italian Community in South Wales, 1881-1945*, Seren, 1991.

James, Brian Ll. edit., *G. T. Clark Scholar Ironmaster in the Victorian Age*, University of Wales Press, 1998.

Jenkins, Geraint H. and Williams, Mari A. edits., *'Let's Do Our Best for the Ancient Tongue', The Welsh Language in the 20th Century*, University of Wales Press, 2000.

Jones, David, and Bainbridge, Alan *The Conquering of China, Crime in an Industrial Community*, Llafur, Volume 2 no. 4, Spring 1979.

Jones, David, *Before Rebecca, Popular Protest in Wales, 1793-1835*, Allen Lane, 1973.

Jones, David, *The Last Rising, The Newport Chartist Insurrection of 1839*, University of Wales Press, 1999.

Jones, Gareth Elwyn, *People, Protest and Politics, Case Studies in 20th Century Wales*, Gomer Press, 1987.

Jones, Glyn *The Island of Apples*, University of Wales Press, 1992.

Jones, Glyn, *The Collected Poems of Glyn Jones, edited by Meic Stephens*, University of Wales Press, 1996.

Jones, Glyn, *The Collected Stories of Glyn Jones, edited by Tony Brown*, University of Wales Press, 1999.

Jones, Glyn, *The Dragon Has Two Tongues*, Dent, 1968.

Jones, Glyn, *The Making of a Poet*, translated from the Welsh by Meic Stephens, Planet, 112 and 113, 1995.

Jones, Jack, *Black Parade*, Faber and Faber, 1935.

Jones, Jack, *Off To Philadelphia in the Morning*, Hamish Hamilton, 1947.

Jones, Jack, *Unfinished Journey (autobiography)*, Oxford University Press, 1937.

Jones, Stephen K., *Brunel in South Wales Vol 1*, Tempus, 2005.

Jones, Wynford, *Class of The 60s, The Stable of Eddie Thomas*, Wynford Jones, 2005.

Kennedy, Ludovic, *Ten Rillington Place*, Gollancz, 1961.

Llewellyn, Carl and Watkins, Hugh, *'Los Desconocidos a L'Extranjero', 'Strangers in a Foreign Land', The Spanish Immigration to Dowlais*, Merthyr Historian Supplementary Edition.

Lord Hartwell, *William Camrose, Giant of Fleet Street, Weidenfeld and Nicolson, 1992. John

McLean, Iain and Johnes, Martin, *Aberfan Government and Disasters*, Welsh Academic Press, 2000.

Merthyr Teachers Centre *Merthyr Tydfil, A Valley Community, 1981*. Merthyr Teachers Centre in conjunction with D. Brown and Sons, Cowbridge.

Merthyr Tydfil and District Naturalists Society, *The Historic Taf Valleys, Vols 1-111*, Merthyr Tydfil and District Naturalists Society, in conjunction with D. Brown and Sons, Cowbridge.

Merthyr Tydfil Borough Council, *Richard Trevithick and the 'Penydarren' Locomotive, Merthyr Tydfil Heritage Calendar*, MTBC, 2004.

Merthyr Tydfil Historical Society, *The Merthyr Historian, Volumes 1-19*, Merthyr Tydfil Historical Society.

Mitchell, Vic and Smith, Keith, *Brecon to Merthyr, Country Railway Routes*, Middleton Press, 2003.

Morris, Brian, *Harri Webb, Writers of Wales series*, University of Wales Press, 1993.

Murphy, Jeff, *Johnny Owen*, Mainstream, 2005.

Norris, Leslie, *Collected Poems*, Seren, 1996.

Norris, Leslie, *Collected Stories*, Seren, 1996.

Norris, Leslie, *Glyn Jones, Writers of Wales series*, University of Wales Press, 1997.

Osborne, Alan, *The Merthyr Trilogy*, Parthian Books, 1998.

Owen, John A, *A Short History of the Dowlais Ironworks*, Merthyr Tydfil Library Service, 2001.

Owen, Wilf, *Dr Thomas Of The Court*, W.B. and T.D. Owen, 2006.

Owen-Jones Stuart, *The Penydarren Locomotive*, National Museum of Wales 1993.

Rattenbury, Gordon and. Lewis, M.J.T, *Merthyr Tydfil Tramroads and their Locomotives*, Railway and Canal Historical Society, 2004.

Rowson, Stephen and Wright, Ian L., *The Glamorganshire and Aberdare Canals*, Black Dwarf Publications, Vol 1, 2001, Vol 2, 2004.

Stanfield, Claude C.B.E, *Stand Up And Be Counted*, T.T.C. Books.

Stephens, Meic, edit., *The New Companion to the Literature of Wales*, University of Wales Press, 1998.

Stephens, Meic, *The Garth Newydd Years*, Planet 83, 1990.

Strange, Keith, *In Search of the Celestial Empire, Crime in Merthyr, 1830-60*, Llafur, Volume 3 no 1 Spring 1980.

Strange, Keith, *Merthyr Tydfil Iron Metropolis*, Tempus, 2005.

Sweet, Philip, *Merthyr Town A.F.C., A History*, T.T.C. Books, 2007.

Taylor, Margaret Stewart, *The Crawshays of Cyfarthfa Castle*, Hale, 1967.

Thomas, Tydfil, *Poor Relief in Merthyr Tydfil Union in Victorian Times*, Glamorgan Archive Service, 1992.

*Valley Lives, Book 2 Boxers and Boxing in the Merthyr Tydfil Valley*, Merthyr Tydfil Libraries, 1997.

Watkins, David, edit., *Magic Moments of Merthyr Tydfil A.F.C.*, David Watkins.

Watkins, David, edit., *Memories of Penydarren Park*, Merthyr Tydfil Supporters Society, 2006.

Webb, Harri, *Collected Poems, edited by Meic Stephens*, Gomer, 1995.

Webb, Harri, *No Half-way House, Selected Political Journalism*, compiled and edited by Meic Stephens, Y Lolfa, 1997.

Webb, Harri, *The Green Desert*, Gwasg Gomer, 1969.

Wilkins, Charles, *The History of Merthyr Tydfil*, 1908 Edition, (CD Rom) Old Merthyr Tydfil.

Williams, David, *The Rebecca Riots*, University of Wales Press, 1986.

Williams, Gareth, *Valleys of Song, Music and Society in Wales 1840-1914*, University of Wales Press, 1998.

Williams, Glanmor, edit., *Merthyr Politics: The Making of a Working-Class Tradition*, University of Wales Press, 1966.

Williams, Glanmor, *Glanmor Williams, a life*, University of Wales Press, 2002.

Williams, Gwyn A., *Fishers of Men, Stories Towards An Autobiography*, Gomer, 1996.

Williams, Gwyn A., *The Merthyr Rising*, University of Wales Press, 1988.

Williams, Gwyn A., , *The Welsh in their History*, Croom Helm, 1982.

Williams, Gwyn A., *When Was Wales? A History of the Welsh*, Black Raven, 1985.

Website: Alan and Geoff's Old Merthyr Tydfil. http://www.oldmerthyrtydfil.com. Indispensable.

# INDEX

# ACKNOWLEDGEMENTS

The fact that so much has been written about the town is both a help and a hindrance for a biographer of Merthyr. If there is an enormous amount of information to call on, the task of separating fact from fiction, truth from worn cliché, offers a demanding challenge. Among the best guides to establishing the facts are those two great historians, namesakes and near-contemporaries, Gwyn Alf Williams and Sir Glanmor Williams. If Charles Wilkins, Merthyr's first biographer, is less reliable, his gift as a storyteller and the vigour of his opinions are undeniable. The nineteen – and still counting – volumes of *The Merthyr Historian* form a unique resource for those interested in the town. The Old Merthyr Tydfil website, with its hundreds of photographs of a Merthyr confined to the memories of a dwindling few, is equally indispensable. I owe a special thanks to Old Merthyr's Alan George. I am the latest in a growing number of writers, television and radio producers and researchers to acknowledge their debt to Merthyr's excellent libraries and to librarian Carolyn Jacob in particular.

Those interested in the psychological and emotional character of the town, as well as its history, must read its great novelists, poets and short story writers, Jack Jones, Glyn Jones, Leslie Norris and the infuriating, stimulating, hugely talented, enfant terrible Harri Webb, a man not born in Merthyr who nevertheless epitomised many of its virtues and its vices. A later generation of writers, including Mike Jenkins and Desmond Barry, have written with passion and perception about the town.

This is a very personal view of Merthyr, seen through the eyes of a sometimes neglectful but always loving son. I want to thank my family and all those friends who made it such a joy growing up in Merthyr. A special thanks to Beti Williams for her insight and support. Her spirit is the true spirit of Wales. Finally, thanks to Peter Finch for trusting me to write this book and to John Owen Thomas for suggesting me.

# THE AUTHOR

Mario Basini was born in Merthyr Tydfil and educated at Cyfarthfa Castle Grammar School. After taking a degree in English at the University College of Wales, Aberystwyth, he taught for a while before joining the *Western Mail* as a journalist in 1967. During 37 years on the newspaper, he did almost every writing job ending as literary editor, chief feature writer and columnist. A former weekly broadcaster on Radio 5 he continues to appear occasionally on Welsh television and more frequently on Welsh radio. His work has appeared in many magazines and in various anthologies. He is a former Welsh Feature Writer of the Year and is an Honorary Fellow of Aberystwyth University.